Developing Narrative Theory

We live in an age of narrative: life stories are a crucial ingredient in what makes us human and, in addition, in determining what kind of human we become. In recent years, narrative analysis has grown and it is now being used across many areas of research. Interest in this rapidly developing approach now requires the firm theoretical underpinning that will allow researchers to both tackle such work in a reliably structured way and interpret the results effectively.

Developing Narrative Theory looks at the contemporary need to study life narratives, considers the emergence and salience of life narratives in contemporary culture, and discusses different forms of narrativity. It shows in detail how life story interviews are conducted, and it demonstrates how the process often begins with relatively unstructured life story collection but moves to a more collaborative exchange, where sociological themes and historical patterns are scrutinized and mutually explored.

At the core of this book the author shows that, far from there being a singular form of narrative or an infinite range of unique and idiosyncratic narratives, there are in fact clusters of narrativity and particular types of narrative style. These can be grouped into four main areas:

- focussed elaborators
- scripted describers
- armchair elaborators
- multiple describers.

Drawing on data from several large-scale studies from countries across the world, Professor Goodson details how theories of narrativity and life story analysis can combine to inform learning potential.

Timely and innovative, this book will be of use to all of those employing narrative and life history methods in their research. It will also be of interest to those working in lifelong learning and with professional and self-development practices.

Ivor F. Goodson is International Professor of Sociology at the University of Tallinn, Estonia, and Professor of Learning Theory in the School of Education at the University of Brighton, UK. He is also Joss Owen Professor at the University of Plymouth and a research associate of the Guerrand-Hermès Foundation for Peace (Paris). For Ivor Goodson's recent publications and activities, his new website can be accessed at www.ivorgoodson.com.

Developing Narrative Theory

Life histories and personal representation

Ivor F. Goodson

 Routledge
Taylor & Francis Group

LONDON AND NEW YORK

First published 2013
by Routledge
2 Park Square, Milton Park, Abingdon, Oxon OX14 4RN

Simultaneously published in the USA and Canada
by Routledge
711 Third Avenue, New York, NY 10017

Routledge is an imprint of the Taylor & Francis Group, an informa business

British Library Cataloguing in Publication Data
A catalogue record for this book is available from the British Library

Library of Congress Cataloging-in-Publication Data
Goodson, Ivor.
Developing narrative theory: life histories and personal representation/
authored by Ivor F. Goodson.
p. cm.
Includes index.
ISBN 978-0-415-60361-4 (hardback) - - ISBN 978-0-415-60362-1 () - -
ISBN 978-0-203-81770-4 () 1. Education- -Biographical methods.
2. Discourse analysis, Narrative- -Research. 3. Postmodernism
and education. I. Title.
LB1029.B55G65 2012
370.72- -dc23
2012012429

ISBN: 978-0-415-60361-4 (hbk)
ISBN: 978-0-415-60362-1 (pbk)
ISBN: 978-0-203-81770-4 (ebk)

Typeset in Bembo
by Integra Software Services Pvt. Ltd, Pondicherry, India

MIX
Paper from
responsible sources
FSC
www.fsc.org FSC® C004839

Printed and bound in Great Britain by the MPG Books Group

For my grandparents, James and
Alice Goodson, their eleven daughters
and their twelfth child, my dad, Fred.
'We're a very persistent family.'

'In the stories people told him he found not only kinship with them but magic and a sense of the unseen.'

C.P. Snow

Contents

List of Figures

Acknowledgements

Thanks to Liz Briggs for her endless good humour, patience and endurance.

Thanks to the research teams in the projects mentioned in Chapter 1, and especially to Martha Foote and Andy Hargreaves on the Spencer project; Teresa Khyasera and Walter Vernon on the REMTEL project; and Anastasia Christou, Janine Givati-Teerling and Russell King on the Diasporas project. Finally, and most influentially, thanks to all of the research team on the most recent project, Learning Lives – especially for the data collection and intellectual collaboration: Norma Adair, likewise Mike Tedder, the other research fellow I worked with, and Gert Biesta, with whom I collaborated closely in the writing of *Narrative Learning*, and who, like all of these colleagues, has influenced the ideas discussed in this book. Research such as that reported here is a cumulative and collaborative process and owes a debt to all of the above.

Thanks also to Mary, my wife, and Andy, my son, with much love.

Part I

Studying Life Narratives

Chapter 1

Introduction: Studying life stories and life histories

Since very early on in my life I have been fascinated by the way people construct and present accounts of their lives. Such life stories fleshed out with anecdotes, jokes and family photos, and often told within family gatherings, were a central part of my upbringing. The fascination was no doubt increased by growing up in a very oral culture, a working-class family with extended community roots.

Mine was a family where the telling of stories was part of our daily living together. It was the main communicative device and a source of enduring pleasure in our family interactions. In a real sense our understanding of the world was constructed and mediated through the stories we shared with each other. Mine was not a world where books featured very centrally. My grandparents could not read or write, and my father, a gas fitter, read using the 'wheelbarrow method' he advocated to all and sundry. Since there were many words he could not read (he left school at 13), he maintained he could get the sense of the meaning by just saying 'wheelbarrow' each time he encountered a word he didn't know. The wheelbarrow method was pioneered by another non-reader he sat next to at school. This boy was famous for telling the headmaster that when he grew up he wanted to be a 'gobbing gardener'. In fact he ended up as one, so the wheelbarrow method also worked for him in the end.

As soon as I learnt to read, at the age of eight, I began to realize that even the literate were highly dependent on stories. Far from being a disadvantage, in some ways my early and rather specialized introduction to the world through stories proved to be enormously helpful. As Christopher Booker's wonderful book details, stories are ubiquitous:

> At any given moment all over the world hundreds of millions of people will be engaged in what is one of the most familiar of all forms of human activity. In one way or another they will have their attention focussed on mental images which we call a story.
>
> We spend a phenomenal amount of our lives following stories: telling them; listening to them; reading them; watching them being acted out on the television screen or in films or on the stage. They are far and away the most important feature of our every day existence.
>
> (Booker 2004: 2)

I believe Booker is entirely correct when he asserts that stories 'are far and away the most important feature of our everyday existence'. For this reason, it has always struck me as surprising, if not downright contrary, that so many of our educational endeavours, whether teaching or learning, pay so little attention to stories. Why are educators so parsimonious in employing the most important feature of our everyday existence? Is there a reason linked to the reproduction of the social order? Are stories too egalitarian, too inclusive, for an educational system that seeks to select and foster certain groups but not others?

In the past three years in the books *Narrative Learning* (Goodson *et al.* 2010) and *Narrative Pedagogy* (Goodson and Gill 2011), a group of colleagues and I have explored the potential of stories, and the narrative techniques underpinning our storied existence, in particular their relationship to different social contexts and varying social purposes.

In a sense, maybe coming to understand the complex juxtaposition of storying and literacy was part of my journey out from my culture, whilst still holding on to its essence. Unlike some scholarship boys, I never at any time had any desire to leave my working-class culture behind. I wanted to travel with it. I was 'coming from the margins' but had no great desire to arrive. A major reason was my enduring fascination with storytelling and my increasing curiosity about people's life stories. An abiding question was: what role do stories play in our life work – in our formulating of plans, dreams, plots, missions, purposes? In short, how efficacious is storying in meaning-making? What ways of knowing are involved in storying? How are 'life stories' implicated in identity, agency and learning?

But, as in life, it is one thing to have a set of questions; it is quite another to have the opportunity to explore them. Our social position also influences our dispositions and capacities. So I have been profoundly fortunate to have the research opportunities to explore my enduring questions about the meaning and status of life stories. Since 1975, I have been involved in a range of university research projects. But I suppose the writing of this book, in one specific sense, echoes a drive to stay close to ordinary working-life culture and not become entirely detached within university academia. It is an attempt to move between my university research into a more broadly conceived and represented set of ideas and to present these ideas in a book form that is not too formally academic, yet is rigorous in its use of evidence and arguments.

A lot of my initial research has been involved with the public sector – the teachers and nurses who provide so much support to our social fabric and social purpose. Investigating their life stories and showing how personal visions and missions mesh with our professional commitments, or clash with those who would restructure their work and missions, has been a research concern of the past three decades. The result has been a series of books in this area: *Teachers Lives and Careers* (Goodson and Ball 1985), *Biography, Identity and Schooling* (Goodson and Walker 1991), *Studying Teachers' Lives* (Goodson 1992), *Teachers' Professional Lives* (Goodson and Hargreaves 1996), *Investigating the Teacher's Life and Work* (Goodson 2008), *Professional Knowledge and Educational Restructuring* in Europe (Goodson and Lindblad 2010).

A lot of my early work was conducted in England and Europe, but in 1986 I went to work in Canada. At that time the country had a strong commitment to the public sector and to public services, whereas Britain seemed intent on dismantling important sections of its social provision. At the same time in Britain, research on social provision and social distribution in the public services was discouraged. The same pattern as that in the early 1980s seems to be reassembling itself under the current British coalition. Perhaps it is not surprising that governments intent on attacking and dismantling the public sector discourage research on its effects.

In the early 1990s, the Social Sciences and Humanities Research Council of Canada adopted a much broader vision of how research could aid our understanding of public affairs. In my case, I was offered funding for a project on the life and work of racial minority immigrant teachers in the country. The work adopted the life history approach, which developed as a means of investigating and illuminating the main issues. Our studies collected a series of life histories and life stories of teachers who were immigrants to Canada and part of racial and ethno-cultural minorities. This was a study which helped me to understand the cultural context of life story work. It is extremely important that life histories focus not just on the narrative of action but also on the historical background, or what I have called 'the genealogy of context'. One of the most detailed studies of narrativity was that of an immigrant from Central America who narrated his story; both as a story of cultural migration and as one of a scholarship boy.

The 'scholarship boy' story (and, of course, there are 'scholarship girl' stories too) is a particular example of a relationship between social structure and story, and how social structures at particular historical times provide available scripts or scripted resources from which people can construct their life stories. The scholarship boy story is a particular example of this juxtaposition of a particular historical moment of opportunity for a selective group of students – sometimes of working-class or minority cultural origin. The storyline then privileges some whilst, of course, silencing others for as long as it is employed. The scholarship boy story was commonly employed in different parts of the world in the 1950s and early 1960s. It was in that sense a socially scripted and sanctioned way to tell a life story, but it also served to underwrite and support a particular moment in history and a particular vision of social opportunity and social structure, and one which at that time distinctly privileged male over female stories. Only recently and retrospectively have scholarship girl stories been given a fair place (for example, Lorna Sage's wonderful *Bad Blood* 2001). To understand such a life story genre properly it has to be read against the backdrop of the historical context which privileges certain storylines. To do that is to move from life story collection to life history construction, whereby the historical context is interrogated and elaborated.

The collection of stories that merely embellish or elaborate mainstream stories, such as that of scholarship boys, essentially stay close to a prior script and in that sense merely fortify patterns of domination. To avoid this in our pursuit of narrativity and to understand it we shall need to move from life stories to life histories, from narratives of action to genealogies of context – in short, towards a way of studying that 'embraces stories of action within theories of context'. If we do this, stories can be 'located', which means they can be seen as the social constructions they are, located in time and space, social history and social geography. Our stories and storylines need to be understood, not just as personal constructions but as expressions of particular historical and cultural opportunities. Life story work concentrates, then, on personal stories, but life histories try to understand stories alongside their historical and cultural backgrounds.

Only if we deal with life stories as the starting point for our understanding, and as the beginning of a process of coming to know, will we begin to understand their meaning. If we use them as starting points we come to see them as social constructions which allow us to locate them in historical time and social space. In this way the life story that is told individualizes and personalizes. But beyond the life story, in the life history, the intention is to understand the pattern of social relations, interactions and historical constructions in which the lives of women and men are embedded. The life history then asks whether private issues are also public matters. It sets our understanding of our life stories within an understanding of the times in which we live and the opportunity structures which allow us to story ourselves in particular ways at particular times.

This broadening of the scope of the Canadian project began to move the focus of my work beyond schooling into other social and cultural locations, and this helped to provide some degree of understanding of how narrativity and personal elaboration change according to particular historical periods and particular cultural locations.

Some of the later work focussed on North America as I was working in Canadian and American universities. In 1998, a considerable grant from the Spencer Foundation allowed a valued team of colleagues and I to use life history methods to explore the histories and practices of the educational endeavour in Canadian and American schools. The studies which emerged in the book *Professional Knowledge, Professional Lives* (Goodson 2003) explored the clash between personal stories and dreams and how these resonated with, or related to, the move towards targets and tests then underway. In American schools they illustrate the profound insensitivity with which new attempts to restructure education dealt with the hopes and dreams of frontline professionals. This clash seems to be heightened amongst the most creative professionals – those who we might assume are in most articulate touch with their own life stories, hopes and dreams.

What then began to emerge in this large research project, involving 18 researchers and a range of schools in two countries, was a pattern of differentiation in the articulation and significance of life stories. Some professionals were clearly very in touch with their own life story and personal vision – it was a matter of intense concern to them and there was a large commitment to the defining and elaboration of their story. These groups seem to find the prescriptive nature of targets and tests highly disruptive and subversive to their sense of purpose. We documented many prize-winning teachers (in America, top teachers often attract a stream of awards) who found the collision between their own story and vision and a micromanaged externally prescribed story and vision traumatic. On the other hand, another group of professionals, especially some of the newer teachers, often accepted external prescription of the story and vision more easily, saying: 'I'm happy to work to the script,' adding 'it's only a job after all.'

This differentiation in the meaning and significance of life stories for professional people began to settle into a new set of questions about life stories. Why do some people spend so much time in interior thought and self-conversation about their life story whilst others seem far less concerned and are willing to accept an externally generated script? Do these different kinds of narrativity crucially affect our identity and agency? Do people's creativity and learning styles respond to these differences? Are there certain historical periods which favour certain kinds of narrativity over others? Were, for example, the 1960s considered special partly because they provided such opportunity for more personalized narrativity, whilst the current period sometimes favours the externally driven prescription of scripts, whether as niche-defined consumers or heavily scrutinized citizens? In short, is narrativity a crucial variable between external structure and personal agency? In understanding narrativity, might we be getting at aspects of a kind of 'DNA of personal response?' To put it in sociological terms, are we looking at a crucial 'mediating membrane' or a 'point of refraction' between external structure and personal agency?

These, then, were some of the questions emerging in the early millennial years as the research studies on professional life stories came to a close. But every pursuit of research questions, especially in the increasingly politicized base of university research, is a victim of serendipity and chance. Here, fortune favoured the pursuit of the questions itemized above. By now, my personal journey had brought me back from America to my much-loved home country with a sense of relief deeply shared by my wife and son. Fortunately, in 2004 two large project grants were awarded, of which I was to be a recipient. As a result, these questions of life stories moved from my personal landscape of concern into the light of seriously funded research scrutiny.

It is always a moment of delicious ambivalence when a new project grant is awarded – one is pleased that personal concerns have become publicly examined issues, but also worried about the scrutiny, unsure of the 'traction' of the ideas, as well as slightly miffed that one's enduring personal preoccupations have been, so to speak, 'outed'.

The two projects that were sponsored neatly joined my previous work on professional life stories with a much broader canvas of investigation. The first, entitled 'Professional knowledge in education and health: restructuring work and life between state and citizens in Europe' (the Professional Knowledge project) (2003–2007), was commissioned by the Education Panel of the European Commission. It was a seven-country, multi-site study covering Finland, Sweden, Ireland, England, Greece, Spain and Portugal. The study collected the life histories or 'work life narratives' of nurses and teachers. These were explored for their significance in response to new 'systems narratives' or governmental reforms. Here, one could see how personal life stories clash, or harmonize, with – or decouple from – government agendas. Without over-simplifying a complex equation, it was certainly possible to see what a vital ingredient the personal life story was in understanding the response to structural, government initiatives. We began to see how the personal story 'refracts' and reinterprets, or sometimes substantially redirects, a governmental initiative. The life story material gave us access to the unpredictable element in social planning. We could see then just how efficacious the 'DNA of the personal response' embedded in the life story was in responding to structural interventions.

The second project got closer to examining the life stories and 'DNA of personal response' by focussing in detail on people's learning across the life course. The Economic and Social Research Council in the UK decided to launch a Teaching and Learning Program. Substantially funded, it aimed to understand how a range of people learn, not particularly in educational institutions but also informally and actively throughout the life course. As a result our own project, entitled 'Learning lives: identity, agency and learning' (the Learning Lives project) (2003–2008), was commissioned. Our intention was to focus on a range of people, encompassing the homeless, asylum seekers, creative artists, members of parliament, and ordinary workers and citizens – in short, a whole spectrum of people covering the multiplicity of English and Scottish society. Having assembled our sample, we then set about collecting exceptionally detailed life stories as a way of understanding people's identity projects, actions and learning. Many of the 160 people whom we spoke to were in fact interviewed for three hours on between six and eight occasions. As a result, we were able to develop a unique archive of just how people understand and narrate their life stories.

At the time when these two large projects were coming to an end, a third project began which also provided fascinating insights into life story material. 'Cultural geographies of counter-diasporic migration: the second generation returns home' (the Diasporas project) (2006–2009), which was funded by the Arts and Humanities Research Board, was a three-year project to study diasporas. As a result, we interviewed second-generation immigrants who were returning to the country of their parents' birth. Whilst this may seem a long way from conventional life history work, it is fascinating in terms of the insights it provides into people's notions of home and national identity. The stories that they tell themselves about home and identity are major influences in how they live their lives. So in this project it is possible to explore once again how narratives lead to plans of action in the real world. Put another way, it is how decisions made in the symbolic universe of a person's story actually feed through into actions in the real world. Adding information from this project to the huge archive generated by the Professional Knowledge and Learning Lives projects provides a rich set of data from which to explore the questions listed above.

In this way, this developing archive of life story interviews was enormously useful for a range of social science purposes. But the particular focus which I want to explore in this book comes back to the question that I mentioned earlier in this chapter: how differentiated are people's patterns of narrativity and is there a way to conceptualize the different styles of narrativity? Further, if we can conceptualize the different kinds of narrative, how relevant are those styles to patterns of identity studies, formation, agency and learning during the life course? We shall see in the rest of this book how a clear pattern of narrativity emerged during the studies, and how several definitive categories of life story and narrativity could be discerned. In the following chapters, the major kinds of narrativity are described and elaborated, and in later chapters the importance of these differences for issues of identity, agency and learning are examined.

Before moving on to the detailed study of narrativity, however, it is important to explain a little about life story methods and to examine the growth of life stories in our cultural life.

Chapter 2

The growth of individual life stories in contemporary life

> When we go on about the big things, the political situation, global warming, world poverty, it all looks really terrible, with nothing getting better, nothing to look forward to. But when I think small, closer in – you know a girl I've just met, or this song we're going to do with Chas, or snowboarding next month, then it looks great. So this is going to be my motto – think small.
>
> (Ian McEwan 2005: 34–35)

There is a kind of popular consensus at the moment that we live in 'an age of narrative'. The truth is rather more complex, for although it is true that narratives and stories are part of the common currency of the day, the scale of those narratives, their scope and aspiration, has dramatically changed. In fact, we are entering a period of particular kinds of narratives: life narratives and small-scale narratives. As McEwan says, increasingly we 'think small'.

In past periods there have been 'grand narratives' of human intention and progress. Hywell Williams, in his study of the chronological history of the world, argues that the link between human history and progress forged into grand narratives grew exponentially in the mid-nineteenth century. He says that the progress narratives that emerged at that time were often 'brash and naïve'.

> It was certainly founded on the fact of material advance – the sudden and greater ease of travel, improvements in sanitation and the reduction in disease, which so impressed contemporaries in the advanced West. These victories also seemed to signify a real moral progress.
>
> Nobody supposed that humanity was getting better at producing saints and geniuses but there was a new confidence in the possibility of a well-ordered society. The intellectual advances that were once the preserve of an educated elite had spread further.
>
> (Williams 2005: 18)

Commenting on the public life associated with these changes, he says:

> Once, the sceptical courtiers of the eighteenth century had sneered at superstition in gossipy little groups – a century later greater masses of people debated great

issues of religion and science, political reform and freedom of trade in public meetings.

(ibid.)

In the last sentence we can see how far public engagement has fallen – the idea of great masses of people debating great issues is inconceivable in the present world. We are more likely to discuss David Beckham's fascinating interior life or Victoria Beckham's opinions than the possibility that we may be entering a new Great Depression with severe implications for all of us. In part, this is closely related to the decline of narrative scope and aspiration. It is also of course related to the growth of political lying (otherwise known as 'spin') – in its way, of course, this is a new kind of storytelling, a new genre of small individualized narratives epitomized in television programmes such as *Who do you think you are?* or Piers Morgan's series of life interviews.

We have witnessed in the twentieth century the collapse of grand narratives. Again, Williams provides a valuable summary:

> The idea of the grand narrative in the human sciences has fallen out of fashion. Christian providence, Freudian psychology, positivist sciences, Marxist class consciousness, nationalist autonomy, fascist will: all have attempted to supply narratives that shape the past. When it comes to practical politics, some of these narratives proved to involve repression and death.
>
> The history of the twentieth century dissolved the connection between material and scientific progress and a better moral order. Technological advance was twice turned, reformed, to the business of mass slaughter in global war, as well as genocide and ethnic cleansing. Material progress was seen to mingle with moral regress. The model T Ford and the gas chamber were the inventions that defined the century.

(ibid.)

We can then begin to see how grand narratives fell from grace, losing not only scope and aspiration but also our underpinning faith in their general capacity to guide or shape our destiny, or render fundamental truths or moral guidance. Into the vortex left after the collapse of the grand narratives we see the emergence of another kind of narrative, infinitely smaller in scope, often individualized – the personal life story. This reflects a dramatic change in the scale of human belief and aspiration. Alongside these small narratives we also see a return to older, more fundamentalist precepts often based on prejudice or ideological assertion.

How has this transformation of the role and scope of narrative come about? How is the new genre socially constructed? Writing in 1996, I argued that literature and art are normally ahead of other cultural carriers of ideology in providing us with new scripts, and in defining our personal narratives and 'life politics'. I said we should locate 'our scrutiny of stories to show that the general forms, skeletons, and ideologies that we employ in structuring the way we tell our individual tales come from a wider culture' (Goodson 2005: 215).

Following this scrutiny, I think we can see in contemporary cultural activity how the move to smaller, more individual life narratives is emerging. Interestingly, this is often referred to as the 'age of narrative'; of narrative politics, of narrative storytelling, of narrative identity. Put in historical perspective, set against the last centuries following the Age of Enlightenment, we should see this as the beginning, not of the 'age of narratives', but of the 'age of small narratives'. In Western countries, particularly in our current individualized society, our art, culture and politics increasingly reflect a move to highly individualized or special interest narratives, which often draw on the literature of therapy and personal and self-development. The narratives are often completely divorced from the wider societal and political context.

Perhaps a few examples from the work of some of our cultural icons will illustrate the point. Bruce Springsteen, the American rock star, has I think always been one of the best and most perceptive storytellers. He writes his songs very carefully and works on quite large canvases of human aspiration at times, such as in his album *The River*. In this album he reflects, in line with Bob Dylan, who recently wrote that he 'hadn't got a dream that hadn't been repossessed', on the limiting of human dreams. Springsteen wrote, 'Is a dream a lie if it don't come true, or is it something worse?' These reflections on the capacity of larger human aspirations to direct our life narratives have been an enduring feature of his work until recently. His album *The Ghost of Tom Joad* profoundly reflects in its title, as well as in its substance, awareness of a massive shift in narrative scope. Tom Joad, of course, the figure in Steinbeck's *The Grapes of Wrath*, carries a storyline linked to mass movements at the time, which aimed to provide social justice at a time of global business depression. Once this link between individual storylines and collective aspirations is broken, we enter the epoch of small narratives, the world of individualized 'life politics'.

In his newer albums, for instance *Devils and Dust*, Springsteen has moved away from references to large historical movements. Sean O'Hagan writes: 'Unlike "The Ghost of Tom Joad" it possesses none of that album's pointed social awareness. Instead we get a set of intimate and often fragmentary glimpses of ordinary people's lives in trouble' (O'Hagan 2005: 7). 'What I have done on this record', elaborates Springsteen, 'is to write specific narrative stories about people whose souls are in danger or are at risk from where they are in the world or what the world is bringing to them' (ibid.).

At certain points, Springsteen tries to link his narratives to a broader tradition, but this time the link is largely rhetorical, for the stories now are fragmentary and individualized without reference to broader social movements (beyond the nebulous 'folk tradition'). As he says, he now writes 'specific narrative stories' about people, and the passivity of the response is reflected in his phrase that these people are 'at risk from where they are in the world or what the world is bringing to them'. The scope and aspiration of narratives is finely elaborated in this quote, and it illustrates the seismic shift in the scope and scale of narrative capacity that has happened over the past two centuries.

The same redefinition of narrative capacity can be seen in film-making. Many film-makers articulate their use of specific life narratives in contemporary film-making.

Jorge Semprun, for example, who has made some of the most resonant political films to come out of Spain, said in an interview that:

> The atmosphere in May 68 and its aftermath created an appetite for political films. But today the mood is different. If you are to make a political film now you have to approach it not from the point of a nation or national struggle, but one of individual choice.
>
> (Interview with Jorge Semprun 2004: 4)

Gil Troy, a history professor writing in *The New York Times*, put it the same way when contemplating the possibilities of action in the contemporary world: 'Our challenge today is to find meaning not in a national crisis, but in an individual's daily life' (Troy 1999: A27).

We see here the changing canvas for narrative construction and the dramatic change in scope and aspiration, and this is reflected in our social and political life. The change can be seen in the political adviser on network television who recently put it this way: 'No it's not that we see the need to change the policy in response to public opposition ... no not at all ... our conclusion is that we need to change the story we tell about the policy.' This statement captures the essence of what we now see in the genre that is emerging as 'narrative politics', or, as Christian Salmon puts it succinctly, 'turning politics into a story' (Salmon 2010). Once this trick is pulled off the story can rise above material reality. So bankers can create a seismic economic collapse, but because similar groups also control the storyline which emerges, this crisis can be 're-storied' as a crisis in the public sector. Economic and political control allows narrative levitation and the promotion of stories as 'a reality'.

This is a perfect redefinition of the new genre of 'narrative politics'. New in one sense, but in fact dating back some way in time – most significantly to the public relations guru, Edward Bernays. Bernays believed it was possible to manipulate people's unconscious desires and by appealing to them you could sell anything – from soap powder to political policies (1924). It was a matter of crafting the right kind of story. Hence:

> You didn't vote for a political party out of duty, or because you believed it had the best policies to advance the common good; you did so because of a secret feeling that it offered you the most likely opportunity to promote yourself.
>
> (Adams 2002: 5)

As Christopher Caldwell has noted as a result of the triumph of narrative politics: 'Politics has gone from largely being about capital and labour to being largely about identity and sovereignty' (2005).

Politicians appear to understand this need for narrative fine-tuning as they hone their policies. The narrative matters more than the substance, as this quote from the late lamented former UK Liberal Democrat leader Charles Kennedy makes clear: 'Whilst we had good and quite popular policies [pause] we have got to find and fashion a narrative' (as quoted in Branigan 2005: 8).

Nothing illustrates the shift from old hierarchies of cultural and symbolic capital towards something we might call 'narrative capital' better than the case of David Cameron, the Tory Prime Minister (see Goodson 2005). In previous generations, his Old Etonian and Oxford connections would have provided an authoritative narrative through which to promote his political ambitions. The cultural and symbolic capital of such an education would then have come with an implicit and very powerful storyline. These places traditionally produced those who govern us whilst their symbolic and social capital was still largely intact. Cameron has predictably worried about constructing an acceptable life narrative which somehow subsumes this old cultural advantage whilst addressing the current needs of the world of narrative politics.

The problem that Cameron faces can be seen in the summary life narrative employed by reporters of the *Daily Mirror*. These were summarized in the *Observer* at the time when Cameron was being closely scutinized for his future leadership potential:

Class Struggle: The Mirror on Cameron

Cameron's all too aware his toff-class membership is a potentially fatal problem, instructing Con spin doctors never to invite your columnist to Tory events, because I've spent 18 months highlighting his toffness. I turn up anyway at Tory shindigs, just to annoy him.

Spotty Cameron was packed off to £25,000-a-year Eton, puffing on wacky baccy rather than learning Latin. Then it was off to Oxford's dreaming spires, where he bought a silly £1,200 tail coat, pratting around as an Edwardian gentleman in the restricted gene pool that is the Bullingdon Club.

Only toffs with plenty of dosh bray there is more to life than money. It's easy for well-heeled David Cameron to come over all Ken Doddish and preach happiness. Daddy was a stockbroker and the Tory leader fought his way to the top from the, er, top. Born with a silver dinner service in his mouth, he suffered the indignity of a bog-standard education at Eton and Oxford.

You don't have to be a toff to get on in Old Etonian David Cameron's Tory Party – but it certainly helps.

Tory toff David Cameron accuses parents who fail to discipline their children of being 'selfish and irresponsible'. But what the hell does Diddy Dave know about that world? His parents didn't raise him like that. They sent him to boarding school as soon as he could say 'Goodbye, Mama'.

Labour MPs were having a fag behind the bike sheds when Tory toff David Cameron was fagging at Eton. The posh chap's latest wheeze to reward youthful goody two-shoes reeks of his privileged upbringing.

(Robinson 2007)

Cameron's awareness of the impending problems was outlined in an early interview with Martin Bertram undertaken before he became leader:

> But as Cameron insists, it is not just his preference for racy television programmes that calls into question the stereotyped image that others have placed upon him. He cites his liking for the 'gloomy left-wing' music of bands such as the Smiths, Radiohead and Snow Patrol, which brings ribbing from his friends, as a further example of his divergence from the traditional Tory image, and also, perhaps rather rashly for a newly appointed shadow Education Secretary, admits to regularly misbehaving 'in all sorts of ways' while at school.
>
> Most importantly, however, he says that what keeps him connected very firmly in ordinary life is the job of representing his constituents in Witney, Oxfordshire, and life at home with his wife, Samantha, and their two children, three-year-old Ivan, who suffers from cerebral palsy and epilepsy, and Nancy, who is aged 14 months.
>
> 'Am I too posh to push?' he quips, before determinedly explaining why he rejects the criticism of his background. 'In the sort of politics I believe in it shouldn't matter what you've had in the past, it's what you are going to contribute in the future, and I think that should be true of everybody, from all parts of society, all colours and ages and races, and I hope that goes for Old Etonians too'.
>
> (Bertram 2005: 10)

What I think Cameron has noted is that if he re-crafts his life narrative 'it shouldn't matter what you've had in the past'. In other words, he is worried that his life experience of sustained, systemic privilege will interfere with the narrative he is trying to create for himself and his party, where there is a 'genuine care and compassion for those who fall behind', and where what 'people really want (is) a practical down-to-earth alternative to Labour'. He ends, 'Am I too posh? It shouldn't really matter where you come from – even if it's Eton.' While Eton, then, may have massive historical claims to cultural and symbolic capital, the narrative capital it provides is clearly a little more difficult to present and cash in. Cameron's honest appraisal of the dilemma elegantly illustrates the seismic shift towards narrative politics and how this is likely to feed through into new educational modes for acquiring narrative capital (see Goodson 2004). These problems with narrative capital have been a gift for humorists. Olly Grender has joked that soon the Tory leader will be claiming that he is descended from a long line of old Etonian goat herders.

It is of course possible that the age of the small narrative might be challenged by cataclysmic external events. The threat of double-dip recession clearly poses problems for the narrative capital of Cameron and Osborne, and for their stress on fairness and the story 'we are all in this together'. This is a difficult story for privileged multi-millionaires to get taken seriously. The same problem will apply to all exhortations to believe we are in the same situation, facing it together. The problem of getting a notion like 'The Big Society' to be taken seriously becomes clear. Cameron lacks the 'narrative capital' for us to believe his story.

In America, the continuation of narrative politics seems stronger than any prospect of change. As usual, Joan Didion put her finger on the essential role of stories in politics in the last presidential election:

> Many had seen a mandate for political change. Yet in the end the old notes had been struck, the old language used. The prospect for any given figure had been evaluated, now as before, by his or her 'story'. She has 'a wonderful story' we had heard about Rice during her 2005 confirmation hearings. 'We all admire her story.' 'I think she's formidable', Senator Biden said about Governor Palin a few weeks ago, 'she has a great story. She has a great family'.
>
> Senator Biden himself was said to have 'a great story', the one that revolved around the death of his first wife and child and taking the train from Washington to Wilmington to be with his surviving children. Senator McCain, everyone agreed, had 'a great story'. Now as then, the 'story' worked to 'humanize' the figure under discussion, which is to say to downplay his or her potential for trouble. Condoleezza Rice's 'story', for example, had come down to her 'doing an excellent job as provost of Stanford' (this had kept getting mentioned, as if everyone at Fox News had come straight off the provost beat) and being 'an accomplished concert pianist'.
>
> Now as then, the same intractable questions were avoided and, in the end, successfully evaded.
>
> (Didion 2008: 2)

The extreme relevance, the enduring and pervasive relevance, of a style of narrativity might be exemplified by the case of Barrack Obama. His life story is well known and has been carefully detailed in his autobiographical books, *Dreams from my Father* (Obama 1995) and *The Audacity of Hope* (Obama 2006). From his earliest days, he has constructed a viable life story from a moving mosaic of figments and fragments. They are in fact astonishingly similar to the case of Bill Clinton – an early sense of life as very precarious with absent fathers and a sense of impermanence which stimulates the child to develop and invent a personal vision of selfhood. This pattern of narrative self-invention thus becomes embedded and becomes a way of being and behaving and becoming. Tim Garton Ash describes it this way:

> You feel this is a man who knows who he is. Not because he has always known who he is like the heir to 'a long line of McCains' but because for a long time he didn't – and then worked it out for himself the hard way, through the search recorded in the autobiographical *Dreams from My Father* he has so to speak, the rootedness of the uprooted.
>
> (Garton Ash 2008: 33)

This has led to a form of narrative intensity that makes the understanding and crafting of political narrative quite literally 'second nature'. His nature is to be in constant narrative process – his whole life he has been at work in the construction of an ongoing life narrative, a narrative identity. Rebecca Walker has reflected upon the relevance of Obama's narrative character to the political work he undertakes:

> America is at the end of one story, and the beginning of another. We are fortunate Obama is a writer. We need his heart and his pen and his intuitive understanding of narrative to bring us to the other side of the current crisis, having learned to turn tragedy – of which we are sure to see more – into insight, and the decline of a superpower into an educational epic of redemption.
>
> We picked the right man for that reason. Not because he's qualified and soulful, which he is, and not because he's committed and brilliant, which he is; but because he knows how to create a phenomenal whole out of a thousand little pieces. It's the story of his multiracial, intercultural, working class, Ivy League, community-organising life. He's been doing it since day one.
>
> (Walker 2008: 36)

As well as his political style, our understanding of his narrative character offers insights into his form of reflexivity: the way he understands, studies and learns. Jonathan Raban has this to say:

> The unique contradictions and messinesses of his own childhood made him an empiricist by instinct, finding a path for himself by testing his footing each step of the way. His education at Columbia and Harvard made him an empiricist by training. As a law professor at Chicago, he pressed his students to adopt contrarian views while playing his own opinions close to his chest. In July this year, the New York Times reported: 'Obama liked to provoke. He wanted his charges to try arguing that life was better under segregation, that black people were better athletes than white ones.' I remember thinking, 'You're offending my liberal instincts', a former student remembered.
>
> In the Illinois State Senate as well as in the US Senate, this has been his habit as a legislator, to solicit counter-arguments against his own position, to deploy his unusual talent as a close and sympathetic listener; to probe, to doubt, to adapt, to change.
>
> (Raban 2008: 29)

The same importance of narrative capital can be seen working its way into the literature on business management and leadership. Peter Senge's (1995) work on the discipline of business leaders points to the salience of what he calls the 'purpose story' in the motivation and direction of business leaders.

To forge the link between the multinational and the personal, we need to grasp each person's life theme. Senge says this about purpose stories:

> The interviews that I conducted as background for this chapter led to what was, for me, a surprising discovery. Although the three leaders with whom I talked operate in completely different industries – a traditional service business, a

traditional manufacturing business, and a high-tech manufacturing business – and although the specifics of their views differed substantially, they each appeared to draw their own inspiration from the same source. Each perceived a deep story and a sense of purpose that lay behind his vision, what we have come to call the purpose story – a larger pattern of becoming that gives meaning to his personal aspirations and his hopes for their organization. For O'Brien the story has to do with 'the ascent of man'. For Simon, it has to do with 'living in a more creative orientation'. For Ray Stat, it has to do 'with integrating thinking and doing'.

   This realization came late one evening, after a very long day with the tape and transcript of one of the interviews. I began to see that these leaders were doing something different from just 'storytelling', in the sense of using stories to teach lessons or transmit bits of wisdom. They were relating the story – the over-arching explanation of why they do what they do, how their organizations need to evolve, and how this evolution is part of something larger. As I reflected back on gifted leaders whom I have known, I realized that this 'larger story' was common to them all, and conversely that many otherwise competent managers in leadership positions were not leaders of the same ilk precisely because they saw no larger story.

   The leader's purpose story is both personal and universal. It defines her or his life's work. It ennobles his efforts, yet leaves an abiding humility that keeps him from taking his own successes and failures too seriously. It brings a unique depth of meaning to his vision, a larger landscape upon which his personal dreams and goals stand out as landmarks on a longer journey. But what is important, this story is central to his ability to lead. It places his organization's purpose, its reason for being within a context of 'where we've come from and where we're headed', where the 'we' goes beyond the organization itself to humankind more broadly. In this sense, they naturally see their organization as a vehicle for bringing learning and change into society. This is the power of the purpose story – it provides a single integrating set of ideas that give meaning to all aspects of a leader's work.

(Senge 1995: 346)

Senge's work epitomizes the kind of management genre that emerged in the mid-1990s and focussed on storytelling. Salmon notes: 'This new school of management emerged in the United States in the 1990s and it recommends bringing "storytellers and griots into companies" ' (Salmon 2010: 32). Steve Denning, one of the gurus, is quoted as saying that 'the origin of my interest in organizational storytelling was simple: nothing else worked' (ibid.). Some economists are beginning to make the same arguments; for example, in the new book *The Romantic Economist*, Richard Bronk asserts:

Politicians would do well to recognise that the main social value of markets in advanced economies may no longer be their ability to engineer increases in wealth, but rather the opportunities they offer individual citizens to develop their own potential, express their identity, and create their own future.

Increasingly, we define our identities by the jobs that we choose to do and the goods that we choose to buy; and, where we are able to do so, we choose jobs and goods that match our idealised visions of the way we wish to live our lives.

(Bronk 2009: 303)

We can see, then, how the 'age of small narratives' and of life narratives has been expressed in emerging patterns of art, politics and business. In this sense, the problematics of studying people's lives are part of a wider context of social relations, priorities and provisions. In the next chapter, we look at the way life stories emerge in particular ways at particular times.

Chapter 3

Contemporary patterns in life stories

The study of personal storylines is one way to examine people's ongoing struggle for purpose and meaning. By scrutinizing storylines in this way, we can begin to understand how the human species is responding to changing historical and cultural circumstances. We will review how historical circumstances have changed in the period of almost 70 years since the end of the Second World War. By seeing how storylines endure over long periods, or are subject to ongoing and precipitous change, we can assess how human meaning-making is responding to changing historical circumstances. Pursuing an analogy with global warming (for, in a sense, both of these contemporary changes emanate from the new juggernaut of globalized commerce), we can judge whether contemporary changes in human storylines are subject to change on a normal scale, or in a seismic epochal manner.

To assess this historical periodization of human storylines, we need to begin with understanding the mode of operation under the last large historical period – the phase we have come to characterize as modernization. Under advanced forms of modernism, a dominant identity project was the construction of a unitary, linear, sequential self, often organized around 'lifetime' commitments to one job and one partner. Associated 'ideologies of significance' created storylines for these lifetime commitments, the notion of 'the career', or of 'romantic love', provided personal flesh for an overriding pattern of societal storylines based on work and family.

Career, as Richard Sennett (1998: 9) reminds us, 'in its English origins meant a road for carriages, and as eventually applied to labo(u)r meant a lifelong channel for one's economic pursuits'. Many now argue that with the move to a new pattern of 'flexible' accumulation, organized globally, such a coherent storyline as the traditional career is unsustainable; the identity project perforce must change. Fernando Flores and John Gray note:

> The career, as an 'institution' is in unavoidable decline. The emergence of knowledge-based economies means the creative destruction of many time-honoured practices, including those at the core of traditional career structures.
>
> (Flores and Gray 2000: 9)

They outline the far-reaching effects of the decline of career, which:

> has been a core social institution of twentieth century industrial civilisation. Though most may never have full access to it, a career has been the most important route to achieving the personal autonomy to which most still aspire. Through careers, people could establish continuity and meaning by being the authors of their economic lives.
>
> (ibid.: 10)

And not just economic lives; the 'career' provided a narrative lynchpin for the authorship of a storyline for a person's life. On the skeleton of 'the career', a whole storyline could be fleshed out, improvised, filled out (we noted earlier how scholarship boys and girls developed their life projects around the career enhancing possibilities offered by their educational mobility). Flores and Gray later concede that the meaning of the decline of careers moves well beyond its economic significance:

> The corrosion of careers has largely been experienced as a diminution of control over one's life [...] The issue people face today is not merely job insecurity, but more the loss of meaning that occurs when working life no longer has a discernible shape.
>
> (ibid.: 11)

If 'career' provided a lifetime storyline for work identity, 'romantic love' often provided a similar script for marriage and family. Philip Knightley has speculated about this: 'At some point, along with tools and language, early man acquired love. Why was it needed? The psychiatrist, Isaac Marks, says that the "lunacy of love" is to bond parents together for the arduous business of raising children' (Knightley 1998: 7). This defence of the storyline of romantic love to provide a meaningful narrative for the business of child-rearing and family has slowly begun to collapse at the same time as modernism's demise. Knightley argues: 'Marriage this century has been based on romantic love. But if romantic love ceases to shore up the couple – and the family – there is nothing to support it except people's desire to believe in marriage. And that, it seems, has simply run out' (ibid.: 7). A literary turning point in the demise of romantic love was undoubtedly the publication of *The Road Less Travelled* by M. Scott Peck in 1978. Peck argued that the concept of romantic love was a myth: even the notion of 'falling in love' was a sham based on sexual desire, not on anything resembling sustained love and commitment. It seems that contemporary opinion agrees with him. Asked in 1998 to list their worries during the next five years, 'a huge majority of those aged 20–34 put not having a steady relationship last. Three-quarters of both sexes said they were more interested in changing jobs than in finding a partner' (Knightley 1998: 7). With similar prophetic inspiration Ian McEwan's book, and the film made from it, *Enduring Love* takes a similarly critical view of romantic love (McEwan 1997).

Once again, the emergence of the new flexible economy seems to have helped to deconstruct one of the established storylines of the past century. But the changing economic patterns and the dissolution of established family structures have substantial implications for social scientific paradigms. Under welfare state modernism, the whole scientific apparatus of the State was linked to the industrial economy and the family. For instance, all the data for the census, the Registrar General's survey categories of social class, are neatly divided into seven occupational groupings. Likewise, data on families provided a central basis for social inquiry and evaluation. So, as well as being a lynchpin for life storylines, these conceptual foci of work, career and marriage were a lynchpin for social scientific investigation and welfare state management. In a sense, the heyday of Western social democracies was underwritten by these storylines.

The new economy is based on flexible accumulation or, in production terms, flexible specialization. This regime of flexible specialization is the opposite of patterns of industrial production in the factory systems of Fordism.

> 'Flexible specialisation' suits high technology: thanks to the computer, industrial machines are easy to reprogram and configure. The speed of modern communication has also favoured flexible specialisation by making global market data instantly available to a company. Moreover, this form of production requires quick decision-making and so suits the small work group. In a large bureaucratic pyramid, by contrast, decision-making can slow down as paper rises to the top for approval from headquarters. The most strongly favoured ingredient in this new productive process is the willingness to let the shifting demands of the outside world determine the inside structure of institutions. All these elements of responsiveness make for an acceptance of decisive, disruptive change.
>
> (Sennett 1998: 12)

The pattern of flexibility in the workforce has a number of incarnations. But broadly it means a sustained move away from an established pattern of employment where the worker was taken on for long durations, often a whole working life, and provided with insurance benefits and pension rights. The latter tended to confirm the worker's 'loyalty' to his employer as well as vice versa. There has been considerable coverage recently of the effect of the erosion of lifelong work on pension rights and benefits, but this is mostly part of a colossal shift to flexible careers. Now a worker may only be employed for specific tasks – say, writing an article, producing a web page, making a carpet. The work is, so to speak, 'put out' to outworkers who are not part of the core employing unit. This unit may just be one entrepreneur, or more likely a company with a small 'core' of workers who manage the flexible workforce to whom work is put out. In an uncanny way, this is quite reminiscent of the major human transformation known as the industrial revolution. Then it was called the 'domestic/putter out system', where a central employing unit 'put out' or contracted out work to be done, often in the home/domestic setting.

These conditions of constant flexibility and disruptive change mean a seismic shift in the way people experience and indeed manage their lives. As people's life worlds are changed, so their life politics also are transformed. By life politics, I mean the array of decisions and negotiations that underpin our lives. Life politics describes the way we manage our lives and encompasses the moral and personal dilemmas and decisions we have to confront. It is, above all, the new conditions for 'life politics' that highlight the changed world in which we now live. For this reason, social science must, with some urgency, move its mode of inquiry and reportage towards the new life worlds people now confront and inhabit.

Given the pioneering, often domineering role of America in framing our new life worlds, it is instructive to look at new work being done there on personal life worlds and life politics. Some of the more innovative psychology being produced by Americans illustrates the historical shift that has taken place. Philip Cushman's work has pointed to the way our conception of self is formed by the economies and politics of particular historical periods. By the self, Cushman means 'the concept of the individual as articulated by the indigenous psychology of a particular group, the shared understandings within a culture of "what it is to be human" ' (Cushman 1990: 599).

Cushman is, I believe, particularly good at characterizing the 'self' that has emerged in America in the post-war era of consumption. He is, therefore, linking our notions of 'self' and one form of life politics to the needs and necessities of the era of consumption. He wants to characterize our 'consuming selves' – the sort of people who are 'constricted' by the requirements of a service economy based on high levels of consumption. He calls the new self of this era the 'empty self', and says that modern America:

> has shaped a self that experiences a significant absence of community, tradition, and shared meaning. It experiences these social absences and their consequences 'interiorly' as a lack of personal conviction and worth, and it embodies the absences as a chronic undifferentiated emotional hunger. The post-World War Two self that yearns to acquire and consume as an unconscious way of compensating for what has been lost: it is empty.
>
> (ibid.: 600)

In some ways, the culmination of the 'empty self' looks like a further stage in the long march of 'individualization'. For over 200 years, Western countries have produced more and more individualized patterns of selfhood. In general, the contemporary, individualized self is a product of modernism, accompanying the development of the new industrial economies which developed from the eighteenth century onwards, and the nation states and welfare states which developed subsequently. The social science paradigms that grew up alongside these developments reflected a belief in objective empiricism, an Enlightenment quest for laws of human nature. The focus of these social scientific quests were the less rooted and communally bound individuals who accompanied the modern state. Social science objectified and quantified these individual members as the modern state sought to control and manage its population.

Many of the tasks of data gathering and social analysis once conducted by social science academics are no longer funded or are handed over to think tanks. These organizations are often closely linked to corporate interests and therefore represent a new aspect of burgeoning 'corporate rule'. The power of corporate rule can be most clearly evidenced in the narrative actions described in Chapter 2.

The accelerating growth of individualization transformed the tasks of social science as the mechanisms of the modern state and modern politics began to recede in the face of the new economy and global consumerism. As Zygmunt Bauman says:

> What the idea of 'individualisation' carries is the emancipation of the individual from the ascribed, inherited and inborn determination of his or her social character [...] To put it in a nutshell, individualisation consists in transforming human 'identity' from a 'given' into a 'task' – and charging the actor with the responsibility for performing that task.
>
> (Bauman 2001: 144)

The transformation of the new global economy transfers the responsibility for individual 'identity' from the group into the hands of the individual. Life politics are thereby projected as being centre-stage, although such politics actually remain somewhat side-stage, for the conditions and parameters for living a life are decided not primarily by the individual but elsewhere. As Bauman says, 'the scope of life politics and the network of forces which determine its conditions, are purely and simply, incomparable and widely disproportionate' (ibid.). So that, therefore, there can be 'biographical solutions to systemic contradiction' (ibid.). He argues that:

> The fast globalisation of the power network seems to conspire and collaborate with a privatised life politics; they stimulate, sustain and reinforce each other. If globalisation saps the capacity of established political institutions to act effectively, the massive retreat from the 'body politic' to the narrow concerns of life politics prevents the crystallisation of alternative modes of collective action on a par with the globality of the network of dependencies. Everything seemed in place to make both the globalisation of life conditions and [...] the atomisation and privatisation of life struggles, self-propelling and self-perpetuating.
>
> (ibid.: 149)

What do life politics and the new globalizing conditions of life mean to the way people now construct their own life stories? The new conditions offer people the chance to author and narrate their own stories, whilst simultaneously circumscribing in new ways their capacity to live their lives autonomously. Locating our studies at the level of life politics and life histories places us at the same intersection of life possibility and circumscribing condition. We enter the same place of possibility and delusion as the individual encounters in the condition of post-modernity. It is a dangerous terrain for the social scientist to inhabit, but as a crucial intersection for observing social action, it is the place to be and to look for some answers to the large questions posed by globalization. How does globalization affect our search for private meaning and public purpose? Will the pervasive inequality that appears to accompany globalization destroy the prospect of amelioration and compassionate social action in public services? Will the spread of the market ultimately destroy the very bases and visions of many people's life stories?

The time of our lives: historical contexts and life stories

'You don't have to like heroes' says Audiard. 'The hero in my film is there to illustrate the capacity for resistance of the individual and his ability to make himself, his own rules, his own life. I like to ask the question: have I just got one life to live or is there another way? And what is the price to pay for that other way, for inventing myself another way – will my second life be more costly than my first?'

(Solomons 2009: 22–23)

The emergence of life stories is of course closely related to the historical construction of notions of selfhood. This can be viewed in the world today if we look at versions of life stories in countries with different patterns of historical and geographic development in the Western world. In some parts of the world, the notion of a private self with an individualized life story may hardly exist. Life can often be 'nasty, brutish and short' and the major concern is understandably survival and basic questions of livelihood. In such circumstances, there is unlikely to be either the time or the inclination for the development of life stories or the more grandiose notions of selfhood. Life stories, then, are intimately connected to cultural locations, to social position and even social privilege as well as to historical periods, which provide different opportunities for the construction and expression of selfhood.

In a way, one might discern a historical model not unlike Maslow's hierarchy of needs (see Chapter 6). In the more historically advanced periods or stages a pattern of what Abraham Maslow calls 'self-actualisation' can be evidenced (Maslow 1954). This pattern is still more easily discerned in the advanced 'Western' countries but it would be a mistake to see 'advancement' and self-actualizing actions as representing more happiness, fulfilment or vitality. Here, the equation is far more complex and needs disentangling through an intriguing and complicated inquiry process. Interestingly, in recent visits to China and South America, as these societies grow in wealth and new elites and middle class groups emerge, I could see more and more work being undertaken on life stories and life histories in universities. This work builds on the growth of life stories emerging in the everyday world of these countries. As countries change their economic and social profiles, so their life story genres change.

This is, however, to point up very clearly that this book is located itself within a cultural context that privileges certain visions of selfhood and life story. It must be firmly acknowledged that the life stories and narratives in this book are collected and analysed within an Anglo-American context and paradigm of selfhood. Our study of human beings in any form, whether it is their narratives or their nature, cannot provide universals, for as Geertz has reminded us, 'there is no such thing as a human nature independent of culture' (Geertz 1973: 49). Geertz's point is made with exemplary clarity: 'there are no generalisations that can be made about man as man, save that he is a most various animal' (ibid.: 40).

Scholars themselves are of course massively implicated in the cultural context and in cultural production. Geertz has pronounced on the implications for anthropologists:

> The major reason why anthropologists have shied away from cultural peculia-rities when it came to the question of defining man and have taken refuge in bloodless universals is that, faced as they are with the enormous variation in human behaviour they are haunted by a fear of historicism, of becoming lost in a whirl of cultural relativism so compulsive as to deprive them of any fixed bearings at all.
>
> (ibid.: 43–44)

The search for 'bloodless universals' is a common theme in scholarship, certainly in government-funded research. But in studying life narratives, this would be the most dangerous of searches to which one could commit.

In previous work, I have talked about the 'internal affairs' of selfhood and narrativity and their 'external relations'. But in many ways this is a false binary and particularly so in the relationship between cultural context, and selfhood and narrativity. The self and the narrative are always produced in interaction with the cultural context – they are social and cultural productions in that sense.

As such, there are no 'bloodless universals' in the study of life narratives. This is not to say that some patternings and clusterings cannot be discerned and that these are not significant. Indeed, this book will present evidence to this effect. But it is to say that these findings are highly culturally contingent. This 'health warning' is not repeated endlessly throughout the book but it holds strong for every assertion and finding presented herein. As Cushman has stated, and I present no caveats or qualifiers to this: 'There is no universal trans-historical self, only local selves [...] no universal theory about the self only local theories' (Cushman 1990: 599).

That having been said, the Anglo-American nexus epitomized in this book is an axis of considerable power in the contemporary world. Whilst there is some evidence of decline, and we may be beyond Wim Wenders' argument that 'America has colonised our unconscious', that power is still pervasive. As countries and their people modernize, they often move towards models of selfhood and narrative that follow a Western model in privileging the contemporary individual over tradition, group or community. That model has privileged individual agency and potential over the forces of contextual inertia, fate, destiny and social structure. These are to be sure Western cultural choices but they have significant influence within the modernizing world.

A story might help to explore this cultural process at work. I was in Beijing in 2008 to lecture on life history methods. The increasing interest in such methods in Asia is no doubt itself indicative of a shifting cultural landscape. On the final day, I let my hosts know that I would appreciate the time and opportunity to walk around their wonderful city. To my immense good fortune I was assigned one of their most brilliant graduate students to show me round. As one does, we chatted away as we wandered through the streets and courtyards (predictably, he spoke perfect English, in contrast to my non-existent Mandarin).

He told me the whole story of his ancestors, of his peasant grandparents and parents. They lived through dramatic times and his stories of their experiences during the Cultural Revolution were vividly recounted. The view was collectively presented, of social classes and regions in flux, of communities in peril and now in prosperity. He, the storyteller, was mostly absent in the account; the individual who walked beside me spoke mainly of others, others embedded in collective milieux and regional settings. I listened intently and shared some information about my own cultural location and my recent homecoming to my own country. At the time, I know I was reflecting on the stark differences in our ways of recounting our stories. After a while, having visited the Summer Palace and other parks and monuments, I grew a little tired – the 40-year age gap began to assert itself. He cautiously asked if I would like a beer. So we sat down outside a café and he ordered a Coca-Cola, whilst I managed to sniff out a yeasty beer. I had been struggling to pronounce my companion's name – 'Gaozheng'. Helpfully, he made me laugh by saying, 'you can call me Rocky'. So I quipped back, 'and does Rocky have a different life story?'

Sure enough he did. And very polished and practised it was. Rocky was an ambitious and talented individual who wanted to develop a cosmopolitan sense of purpose and travel to England. His story of his learning and education took him from a poorly resourced local school to a secondary school 500 kilometres from home and on to his current highly prestigious scholarship at Beijing Normal University. This was a recognizable scholarship boy story of individual application and talent taking him out into the cosmopolitan world of Beijing's internationally focussed university and from there to an ambition to study in England.

In due course, he was able to come and work with me in England but always seemed able to hold both kinds of storyline together – switching between the more tradition-bound ancestor account and the individualized scholarship boy story. As an example of the transitions in Chinese society, this example seems instructive, although not (bloodlessly) universal. As China modernizes, it is to be expected that more Westernized storylines might emerge and might sit alongside more traditional collective accounts.

The Anglo-American versions of selfhood and narrative are culturally contingent, but the continuing powers of the cultural productions (from Hollywood to hip-hop) of this script do influence emerging visions of self-narrative in other cultural locations. How this works out in each cultural context is through a process of cultural translation and refraction. The local and personal can refract and re-frame, and by focussing on life narratives we can study this process at work. By focussing on changing historical circumstances we can discern some of the processes at work.

Of course, changes in the everyday world can be scrutinized in the private domain of people's lives. Lasch, for instance, has scrutinized the historical trajectory of private lives in *Haven in a Heartless World* (Lasch 1977). In his history of modern society he discerns two distinct phases. In the first phase, he argues that the division of labour that accompanied the development of individual capitalism deprived ordinary people of control over their work, making that work alienating and unfulfilling. In the second phase, Lasch argues that liberalism promoted a view that, while work might be alienated under capital, all could be restored in the private domain. 'It was agreed that people would be freed to pursue happiness and virtue in their private lives in whatever manner they chose.' The workplace was this severed form where work was alienated and heartless; the home and the family became the 'haven in the heartless world' (Menaud 1991).

No sooner was this equation established, Lasch argues, than liberalism reneged.

> Private life was opening up to the 'helping' professions: doctors, teachers, psychologists, child guidance experts, juvenile court officers, and the like. The private domain was immediately made prey to these quasi-official 'forces of organized virtue' and 'the hope that private transactions could make up for the collapse of communal traditions and civic order' was smothered by the helping professions.
>
> (Lasch 1977: 168)

Interestingly, Denzin (1991) has argued that ethnographers and biographers represent the latest wave in this 'penetration' of private lives, and that this is to be expected at a time when we see 'the emergence of a new conservative politics of health and morality, centring on sexuality, the family and the individual' (ibid.: 2). Hence, he argues:

> The biography and the autobiography are among Reagan's legacy to American society. In these writing forms the liberal and left American academic scholarly community reasserts a commitment to the value of individual lives and their accurate representation in the life story document. The story thus becomes the left's answer to the repressive conservative politics of the last two decades of American history. With this method the sorrowful tales of America's underclass can be told. In such tellings a romantic and political identification with the downtrodden will be produced. From this identification will come a new politics of protest; a politics grounded in the harsh and raw economic, racial, and sexual edges of contemporary life. This method will reveal how large social groupings are unable to either live out their ideological versions of the American dream, or to experience personal happiness.
>
> (Denzin 1991: 2)

And further:

> In re-inscribing the real life, with all its nuances, innuendoes and terrors, in the life story, researchers perpetuate a commitment to the production of realist, melodramatic social problems texts which create an identification with the downtrodden in American society. These works of realism reproduce and mirror the social structures that need to be changed. They valorise the subjectivity of the powerless individual. They make a hero of the interactionist-ethnographer voyeur who comes back from the field with moving tales of the dispossessed.
>
> (ibid.: 2)

The rise of the life narrative clearly comes with a range of problems, but also possibilities for the social scientist. By scrutinizing the wider social context of life narratives, we can begin to appreciate the dilemmas of that qualitative work which focusses on personal narratives and life stories.

The version of 'personal' that has been constructed and worked for in some Western countries is a particular version, an individualistic version, of being a person. It is unrecognizable in some parts of the rest of the world. But so many of the stories and narratives that have been developed employ, unproblematically and without comment, this version of personal being and personal knowledge. Masking the limits of individualism, such accounts often present 'isolation, estrangement and loneliness [...] as autonomy, independence and self-reliance' (Andrews 1991: 13). Andrews concludes that if we ignore social context, we deprive ourselves and our collaborators of meaning and understanding. She says, 'It would seem apparent that the context in which human lives are lived is central to the core of meaning in those lives', and argues, 'researchers should not, therefore, feel at liberty to discuss or analyse how individuals perceive meaning in their lives and in the world around them, while ignoring the content and context of that meaning' (ibid.: 13).

The truth is that often a life storyteller will neglect the structural context of his or her life, or interpret such contextual forces from a biased point of view. As Denzin says, 'Many times a person will act as if he or she made his or her own history when, in fact, he or she was forced to make the history he or she lived' (Denzin 1989: 74). He gives an example from the 1986 study of alcoholics: 'You know I made the last four months, by myself. I haven't used or drank. I'm really proud of myself. I did it' (ibid.: 74–75). A friend, listening to this account commented:

> You know you were under a court order all last year. You know you didn't do this on your own. You were forced to, whether you want to accept this fact or not. You also went to AA and NA. Listen Buster you did what you did because you had help and because you were afraid, and thought you had no other choice. Don't give me this, 'I did it on my own' crap.

The speaker replies, 'I know. I just don't like to admit it.' Denzin concludes:

> This listener invokes two structural forces, the state and AA, which accounted in part for this speaker's experience. To have secured only the speaker's account, without a knowledge of his biography and personal history, would have produced a biased interpretation of his situation.
>
> (ibid.: 74–75)

The great virtue of stories is that they particularize and make concrete our experiences. This, however, should be the starting point in our social and educational study. Stories can so richly move us into the terrain of the social, into insights into the socially constructed nature of our experiences. Feminist sociology has often treated stories in this way. As Hilary Graham says, 'Stories are pre-eminently ways of relating individuals and events to social contexts, ways of weaving personal experiences into their social fabric' (see Armstrong 1987: 14). Again, Carolyn Steedman speaks of this two-step process. First, the story particularizes, details and historicizes – then at second stage, there is an 'urgent need' to develop theories of context:

> The fixed townscapes of Northampton and Leeds that Hoggart and Seabrook have described show endless streets of houses, where mothers who don't go out to work order the domestic day, where men are masters, and children, when they grow older, express gratitude for the harsh discipline meted out to them. The first task is to particularize this profoundly a-historical landscape (and so this book details a mother who was a working woman and a single parent, and a father who wasn't a patriarch). And once the landscape is detailed and historicized in this way, the urgent need becomes to find a way of theorizing the result of such difference and particularity, not in order to find a description that can be universally applied (the point is *not* to say that all working-class childhoods are the same, nor that experience of them produces unique psychic structures) but so that the people in exile, the inhabitants of the long streets, may start to use the autobiographical 'I', and tell the stories of their life.
>
> (Steedman 1986: 16)

The story, then, provides a starting point for developing further understandings of the social construction of each person's subjectivity. If the stories stay at the level of the personal and practical, we forego that opportunity. Speaking of the narrative method focussing on personal and practical teachers' knowledge, Willinsky writes: 'I am concerned that a research process [that] intends to recover the personal and experiential would pave over this construction site in its search for an overarching unity in the individual's narrative' (Willinsky 1989: 259).

These, then, are the issues that begin to confront us as the age of the life narrative gathers pace. Let us then review some of the problems that people working with individual life narratives face. First, the personal life story is an *individualizing* device if divorced from context. It focusses on the uniqueness of individual personality and circumstance, and in doing so may well obscure or ignore collective circumstances and historical movements. Life stories are only constructed in specific historical circumstances and cultural conditions – these have to be bought into our methodological grasp.

Second, the individual life story, far from being personally constructed, is itself *scripted*. The social scripts people employ in telling their life stories are derived from a small number of acceptable archetypes available in the wider society. The life story script, far from being autonomous, is highly dependent on wider social scripts. In a sense, what we get when we listen to a life story is a combination of archetypal stories derived from wider social forces and the personal characterizations the life storyteller invokes. The life story therefore has to be culturally located as we pursue our understandings.

In general, life stories themselves do not acknowledge this cultural location explicitly; neither do they reflect explicitly on their historical location in a particular time and place. The life story as data, therefore, faces a third dilemma in that it can be a *de-contextualizing* device, or at the very least an under-contextualizing device. The historical context of life stories needs to be further elucidated, and they need to be understood in relation to time and periodization. We can think of time, as the French Annalistes do, as existing at a number of levels.

First, there is broad historical time – the large sweeps and periods of human history – that the Annalistes called the *'longue durée'*.

Then there is generational or cohort time – the specific experiences of particular generations – say, the 'baby boomers' born after the Second World War.

Then there is cyclical time – the stages of the life cycle from birth through to work and child-rearing (for some) through to retirement and death.

Finally, there is personal time – the way each person develops phases and patterns according to personal dreams, objectives or imperatives across the life course.

These three features of life story narrative – their individual focus, their capacity to reiterate social scripts and their relationship to the historical time zones and social milieux in which they are embedded – all imply a need for life history study. We have to move from the collection of individual life stories towards a method that investigates the social and historical context in which these stories are enmeshed. A life story is poised between personal and individual and social/historical production. As we shall see, the nature of this balance relates to different kinds of narrativity.

By moving our methodological focus from life stories to life histories, we can begin to redress the dangers of individualization and social and historical de-contextualization. The life history explores the interface between the individual representation and the social and historical forces impinging on these representations.

These historical factors associated with time and period have to be addressed as we develop our understandings of life story data. The aim is to provide a story of individual action within a theory of context. This aim is served when we make the transition from life story studies to life histories. In the process, the life story is located within the broader historical context. In the next chapters we shall examine this process in further detail.

Chapter 4

Life histories and personal representation

We have come to see how vital it is to understand life stories in their historical and cultural settings if we are to investigate and understand individual and personal meaning-making. In this chapter, I set out to explain the tradition of life history work and its importance in understanding life stories in their historical context.

If we go back in time, the life history method began as a serious form of study in the early nineteenth century. The first people to use detailed life histories were anthropologists who studied the autobiographies of Native American chiefs – for example, Barrett (1906) and Radin (1920). Since that time, a range of other studies have emerged by sociologists and other scholars, mostly working in the humanities, who have increasingly used a life history approach. Over the years, the popularity and acceptance of life history methods has of course waxed and waned. A particular period of popularity was the 1920s and 1930s, when economic conditions made an understanding of people's life stories within the historical context particularly important. In significant ways, this is a period with many similarities to the economic conditions of the contemporary world. These conditions make it highly likely that there will be a major renaissance of life history studies in the current conjuncture.

Some of the most important life history studies were conducted at the Chicago School of Sociology. Books that focussed on the emerging urban environment of Chicago included *The Gang* (Thresher 1928), *The Gold Coast and the Slum* (Zorbaugh 1929), *The Hobo* (Anderson 1923), *The Ghetto* (Wirth 1928) and Shaw's magnificent account of a mugger called *The Jack-Roller* (Shaw 1930). All employed life history methods.

Howard Becker, an important advocate of life history methods, comments on Shaw's story of the jack-roller in a way that highlights the major strengths of the life history method. The jack-roller in question is called Stanley, and Becker says that:

> By providing this kind of voice from a culture and situation that are ordinarily not known to intellectuals generally and to sociologists in particular, *The Jack-Roller* enables us to improve our theories at the most profound level: by putting ourselves in Stanley's skin, we can feel and become aware of the deep biases about such people that ordinarily permeate our thinking and shape the kinds of

problems we investigate. By truly entering into Stanley's life, we can begin to see what we take for granted (and ought not to) in designing our research – what kinds of assumptions about delinquents, slums and Poles are embedded in the way we set the questions we study.

(Becker 1970: 71)

Conducted successfully, the life history forces a confrontation with other people's subjective perceptions. This confrontation can be avoided, and so often is avoided, in many other social scientific methods: one only has to think of the common rush to the quantitative indicator or theoretical construct, to the statistical table or the ideal type. This sidesteps the messy confrontation with human subjectivity, which I believe should comprise the heartland of the sociological enterprise. Behind – or coterminous with – this methodological sidestep, there is often a profound substantive and political sidestep. In the avoidance of human subjectivity, quantitative assessment and theoretical commentaries can so easily service powerful constituencies within the social and economic order. This tendency to favour and support existing power structures is always a potential problem in social science. Life history studies can also be colonized in this way, and it is vital that we employ life history methods in ways that speak the truth to power structures with regard to the historical contexts of people's lives. This point is well addressed by Becker.

From the statement about 'putting ourselves in Stanley's skin', Becker went on to assert that Stanley's story offered the possibility 'to begin to ask questions about delinquency from the point of view of the delinquent' (Becker 1970: 71). From this, it followed that questions will be asked, not from the point of view of the powerful actors, but rather from the perspective of those who are 'acted on in' professional transactions. These are some of the important reasons why, beyond the issues of methodological debate, life history methods might be unpopular in some quarters. Life history, by its nature, asserts and insists that power should listen to the people it claims to serve, as Becker noted:

If we take Stanley seriously, as his story must impel us to do, we might well raise a series of questions that have been relatively little studied – questions about the people who deal with delinquents, the tactics they use, their suppositions about the world, and the constraints and pressures they are subject to.

(ibid.: 1970)

However, this contention should be read in the light of Shaw's (1930) own 'early warning' in his preface, where he cautioned the reader against drawing conclusions about general causes of delinquency on the basis of a single case record.

One of the best early attempts to analyse the methodological base of the life history method was Dollard's *Criteria for the Life History* (1949). Foreshadowing Becker, he argued that 'detailed studies of the lives of individuals will reveal new perspectives on the culture as a whole which are not accessible when one remains on the formal cross-sectional plane of observation' (Dollard 1949: 4). Dollard's arguments have a somewhat familiar ring, perhaps reflecting the influence of George Herbert Mead. Dollard noted that:

> as soon as we take the post of observer on the cultural level the individual is lost in the crowd and our concepts never lead us back to him. After we have 'gone cultural' we experience the person as a fragment of a (derived) culture pattern, as a marionette dancing on the strings of (reified) culture forms.
>
> (ibid.: 5)

In contrast to this, the life historian 'can see his [sic] life history subject as a link in a chain of social transmission' (ibid.: 5). This linkage should ensure that life history methods will ameliorate the 'presentism' that exists in so much sociological theory and a good deal of symbolic inter-actionism. Dollard described this linkage between historical past, present and future:

> There were links before him from which he acquired his present culture. Other links will follow him to which he will pass on the current of tradition. The life history attempts to describe a unit in that process: it is a study of one of the strands of a complicated collective life which has historical continuity.
>
> (ibid.: 15)

Dollard was especially good, although perhaps unfashionably polemical, in his discussion of the tension between what might be called the cultural legacy, the weight of collective tradition and expectation, and the individual's unique history and capacity for interpretation and action. By focussing on this tension, Dollard argued, the life history offers a way of exploring the relationship between the culture, the social structure and individual lives. Thus, Dollard believed that in the best life history work:

> we must constantly keep in mind the situation both as defined by others and by the subject, such a history will not only define both versions but let us see clearly the pressure of the formal situation and the force of the inner private definition of the situation.
>
> (ibid.: 32)

Dollard saw this resolution, or the attempt to address a common tension, as valuable because 'whenever we encounter difference between our official or average or cultural expectation of action in a "situation" and the actual conduct of the person this indicates the presence of a private interpretation' (ibid.: 32).

In fact, Dollard was writing in 1949, some time after a decline set in for life history methods (an unfortunate side effect of which is that Dollard's work is not as well known as it should be). After reaching its peak in the 1930s, the life history approach fell from grace and was largely abandoned by social scientists. At first this was because the increasingly powerful advocacy of statistical methods gained a growing number of adherents among sociologists but perhaps it was also because, among ethnographically inclined sociologists, more emphasis came to be placed on situation rather than on biography as the basis for understanding human behaviour.

Becker's argument goes to the heart of the contemporary appeal of life history methods. But what Becker is saying is that life history data disrupt the normal assumptions of what is known by intellectuals in general and social scientists in particular. When conducted successfully, the life history method forces us to confront other people's subjective perceptions. At this time, in an individualized, postmodern society this confrontation is absolutely crucial to our understanding of the world. However, as can be seen with many of the studies that still pass for intellectual work, this confrontation between our understanding of the world and other people's can easily be avoided. If we look at a wide range of government studies across the Western world, the way that this confrontation with other people's experience and understanding of the world is avoided is by the common rush to the quantitative indicator or theoretical construct, to the statistical table or the ideal type. One only has to think of government targets and tests as classic examples of this rush to the quantitative. What the quantitative in these cases does is obscure the social experiences and social conditions of the people who are presented by the aggregate number in the table. In this way, political and social indicators are divorced from the social realities they are supposed to represent. Life history studies try to put people's subjective experience back into the equation so that we can begin to understand why it is that people feel about the world and talk about the world and tell stories about the world in the way that they do.

In the contemporary world, we have argued that individual life stories are a growing form of representation and that life history methods have once again become critically important ways of understanding these presentations. As Munro has argued:

> The current focus on acknowledging the subjective, multiple and partial nature of human experience has resulted in a revival of life history methodology. What were previously criticisms of life history, its lack of representativeness and its subjective nature, are now its greatest strength.
>
> (Munro 1998: 8)

This is why, in trying to explore the various questions about life stories posited in the previous three chapters, I have employed life history methods. To explain this a little further, let me take one of the projects mentioned in Chapter 1 that employed life history studies to understand people's lives and the stories they tell about them. The Learning Lives research project began in 2004 and ran until 2008. The project was a collaboration between a number of universities based at Exeter, Brighton, Leeds and Stirling. Learning Lives was a longitudinal study which aimed to deepen our understanding and meaning of the significance of learning in the lives of adults and of how the life stories that adults told expressed their understandings. The focus of the research was on the interrelationship between people's learning lives, their identities and their actions. There were a number of strands in the data collection for the project. For instance, there was a large data set of 10,000 adults who were reviewed quantitatively using the British Household Surveys. There were also studies of people's life courses. But the section that I want to use here to exemplify life history work was the section that I was most involved with. This was a qualitative study using life history methods of around 160 people drawn from different walks of life, living in different parts of the country and of different ages, genders and ethnicities.

Collecting people's life histories

In our project at Brighton we were able to interview a wide range of people: farmers, housewives, retired business people, asylum seekers, homeless people, through to members of the House of Lords and quite well known creative artists. This range of human data collection allowed us to get a sense of how widely differentiated people's storytelling was, and how a patterning of particular types of narrativity emerged. In the following chapters, the types of narrativity that emerged are described and evaluated, but for the moment I want to explain how life history material is collected and the way in which this helps us to understand the way people tell their life stories.

In the Learning Lives project most of our interviews took between two and three hours and we interviewed many of our respondents between six and eight times. Our intention in the first interview was to very much favour the life story the person wanted to tell. This meant almost taking 'a vow of silence' as an interviewer. It was judged that the more we questioned and structured the interview, the less likely we were to encounter the life story that the person was working with and constructing in an ongoing manner. This is an intensely important starting point of all life history work – it has to be the life story as experienced and represented by the storyteller. Often, this life story is quite well rehearsed, for as storytelling animals many human beings already have their life story well worked out before any interviewer appears on the scene! One of the most common questions asked about life story interviews is, how do you get people to tell their life story? Having done a lot of this work, my answer to that would be, how do you get people to stop telling their life story?

Before providing more details about life history interviews, it is worth providing a small health warning. Most life history interviews proceed unproblematically, but people's interest in what happens to the interview is not always quite as the interviewer might hope. Take, for instance, one potential interviewee Teddy's response to a request for an interview from an American academic:

> You fucking come and see me, fucking write about me, you fucking long streak of fucking useless – come and put this in a fucking book, fucking professor, fucking Thunderbird's brains.

> (Campbell 1996)

In spite of Teddy's mild opposition to life history interviews, most of our life story interviewees were positive about being involved.

There are of course many ways to conduct life story interviews, but in the preparation of life history interviews there are a number of stages in the development of the study.

Thus, interviews began as very unstructured with very few questions, but as the project progressed and an initial analysis was undertaken so a progressive focussing and some degree of structure began to take place in the 'grounded conversation' of the life story interview and in the questions asked on both sides of the encounter.

The desire to keep interviews unstructured at the beginning arose from a desire to get the life storytellers to rehearse their story with us, with as little intervention as possible. The role of the interviewer was one of listener, and we tried, at least in the first interview, to keep as close as we could to our 'vow of silence'.

As the next interviews progressed, our interview questions were based on the original, largely unquestioned, life story. As the interviewer began to cross-question the life storyteller using other data sources, such as documentary data and other testimonies, we moved from life story to life history. The process of triangulation represents this move to life history. This is a much more elaborate, two-way encounter than the first interview.

The life history can be seen as the 'triangulate' created from the original life story by employing documentary and oral data on historical context and other oral testimonies (Figure 4.1). If, for instance, a life storyteller is recounting their experiences in the 1960s a range of other documentary and oral data is available to develop their evocation of that historical period. By bringing in these data, a more comprehensive commentary on the historical context can be collaboratively developed. The life storyteller, in collaborating on the elaboration of the historical context, begins to place or 'locate' his or her life story in a particular time and place.

The move from life story to life history involves a complex methodological understanding – more than can be provided in this short section. This methodology has been explored in detail in a range of other books. For instance, with Pat Sikes

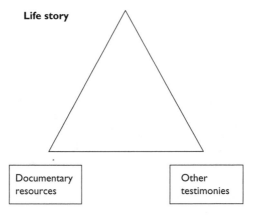

Figure 4.1 The life history

I have provided an introductory text on how life history methods are employed in studying educational settings (Goodson and Sikes 2001), and with Scherto Gill a more extensive discussion of life history methods in narrative research (Goodson and Gill 2011). But the range of work on life history is extensive and can easily be accessed in the bibliographies of these and many of the books on narratives and qualitative methods.

How, then, did we organize our work to make sure that our collection of life narratives did not fall into the traps of individualization, scripting and de-contextualization? The answer is that we tried to build in an ongoing concern with time and historical period, and context and social location.

This meant that our initial collection of life stories as narrated moved on to become a collaboration with our life storytellers about the historical and social contexts of their lives (Figure 4.2). By the end, we hoped that the life story would become the life history because it was located in historical time and context – our sequence then moved in this way:

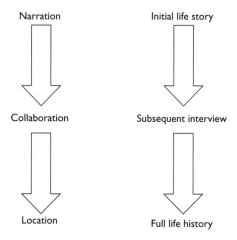

Figure 4.2 Developing life history interviews

Let me give one concrete example of how location might work in some of our research studying teachers' lives. In the life stories of teachers nowadays the normal storyline is one of technicians who follow government guidelines and teach a curriculum that is prescribed by governments or departments of education. The storyline therefore reflects a particular historical moment where the teacher's work is constructed in a particular way. If, however, one compares current teacher storylines in England with the storylines collected 30 or 40 years ago, those stories are of professionals who had autonomy and the capacity to decide what curriculum to teach and what content to include to carry that curriculum. Now in seeking to locate the life story of current teachers, we had to collaborate about the ongoing construction of teachers' work in a particular way. In coming to understand how contemporary teachers' work is provided by a particular work context, our collaborations also provided some sense of the historical context of teachers' work and how this has been subject to change and transition as the historical circumstances of schooling has changed. Hence, in moving from narration through to location, a historical understanding of teachers' work might emerge in the ongoing narrative interviews and collaborations.

The move from life story to life history is a crucial watershed in collaborative narrative interviews. But the stages do not unfold uniformly or in similar sequence for each narrative interview. By exploring the juxtaposition of life story and historical context, we are drawn to an understanding of how people's narrative character is differentiated. In Chapter 6 we begin to address this complex conundrum.

Chapter 5

Developing narrative portrayals

In Chapter 4, there are initial descriptions of the underpinning life history methodology employed in much of the research represented herein. Life history interviews are a perfect vehicle for exploring the complexity of people's personal narratives. As explained in Chapter 4, the collection and collaboration at the heart of life history interviews stressed the life story narration as a starting point. We showed how subsequently a 'progressive focussing' takes place and a grounded conversation begins to take over, which elicits information about the historical context and social location.

Life history interviews provide a wealth of data – in some cases we conducted six or even eight three-hour interviews with life storytellers. A large data bank of interview transcripts can be generated in this way, and the process of analysing these data is inevitably painstaking and complicated. There are various computer aids and packages that can help, from the simple use of 'keywords' through to programmes such as QualiData or Ethnograph. These can help considerably in identifying some of the most generative interviews and some of the most representative life storytellers.

My personal preference, however, is for a more manual process I call 'bathing in the data' (some might say 'drowning in the data' and it may feel like that at the beginning!). This means reading through the transcripts in a slow, incremental manner. Whilst doing this I keep a 'thematic notebook', marking out the main emergent themes in the notebook and on the transcript pages. Over time, some themes become 'saturated' – that is, they occur commonly and are clearly salient points in many life stories (for a detailed presentation of these points, see Chapter 2, Goodson and Sikes 2001).

As themes emerge from the detail of life history interviews, it becomes clear that some life storytellers cover many of the relevant themes, whilst others may only contain evidence of a small number of themes or may cover the themes superficially or rapidly. I use the phrase 'thematic density' to characterize those life history interviews that either cover a wide range of themes or cover particular themes in deep and profound ways.

Having then identified the major themes at work in life narratives, and having begun to employ some of these themes to conceptualize narrative character, a new stage of work can be undertaken. In many of the research studies I have been involved in, I have advocated and employed the development of detailed personal case studies or 'portrayals of the most thematically dense' life histories. The portrayal stage represents a second stage in the focussing of the data from the earlier stages, and transcription and transcript analysis to develop thematic understandings. The portrayal refines these general thematic analyses and presents them in the form of a detailed individual portrait of a life narrative.

In the following chapters, these portrayals and the foregoing thematic analysis that confirms their representativeness provide the data base for the conclusions about narrative character. As a way of characterizing the portrayal genre, the following study of Eva illustrates a portrayal that I developed in the early stages of the Learning Lives project. The portrayal method was highly influential in some of our findings presented in the book *Narrative Learning* (Goodson *et al.* 2010). However, in the book the focus is specifically on learning. In this portrayal, a more general thematic emphasis is employed, which allows us to glimpse a way of studying narrativity.

From the beginning, Eva was enthusiastic about talking to us on the Learning Lives project. Before the interview, we had a number of exploratory conversations and talked a good deal about the project and how life history interviews are conducted. It was clear that these interviews would fit into Eva's ongoing sense of curiosity and inquiry about the world and her place within it. I have presented this portrayal in its original roughness to show how interview data 'feel' when first collected and how initial attempts to theorize and contextualize these data, and to develop a life history perspective, are collaboratively generated between interviewer and interviewee. Life history knowledge is generated socially and collaboratively within the interview setting and the research team milieu. In Eva's case, it can be seen clearly just how active she, the life storyteller, was in developing theories and themes about her own life.

Eva Freud: developing a portrayal

Eva Freud was born in Romania, in a Transylvanian city that often changed hands from the Austro-Hungarian Empire period onwards. In 1971, when she was born, the city was a site of shifting loyalties and allegiances, with changing ethnic identities a part of its modern cultural and political history. Her mother is 'Jewish Hungarian, brought up in Germany and Hungary', her father 'Catholic, very Hungarian'. Both parents were musicians. Eva's father:

> was very involved with other intellectuals trying to counteract the cultural repression of Hungarians at that time in Romania, and for that there's been a bit of trouble with local security services and so on. So, for example, he wasn't given a passport to travel to see his only brother … who ran way to Finland. He was refused a passport because he was politically active.

This Hungarian background set up from the beginning a difficulty with issues of becoming and belonging:

> We grew up very much in an environment where we knew that, erm, that we hear at home we should not replicate, erm, in the street because it'll be, it'll mean serious trouble for my parents. Erm, I was brought up in, erm, to speak Hungarian until the age of six, and that was interesting because basically we should have been bilingual because the country's language is Romanian, erm, but because my parents' allegiance, erm, my father was very adamant that we should learn proper literary Hungarian first and nothing else, so therefore when I was in the street and someone said in Romanian, 'Hey, are you a girl or a boy?' because I used to be a bit of a tomboy, erm, I used to very proudly reply in Romanian, 'I do not speak Romanian'.

The split between living in Romania and being Hungarian was replicated by the split between the Hungarian nationalist allegiance of her father and her mother's Jewish identity.

> I suppose from my father's, you know, friends and circle, erm, and there was a very strong knowledge that the state wanted us Hungarians not to have our culture, erm, that, er, culturally, for example, my parents worked in an opera house, and in the early 1980s two, at least two pieces which were, it was a Hungarian opera house, it was the only one in the country that performed in Hungarian, and it was like the ENO here, that everything was performed in Hungarian, Italian operas, German operas and so on, and there were about two or three pieces on the repertory which the public always flocked to and they were nineteenth-century Hungarian written operas which was very much, which were very much influenced by the 1848 Revolution, erm, and those were forbidden. Those were taken off the repertoire and that was that. So as a, as a consequence the public, for example, did this kind of silent, erm, erm, protest in the famous Slave's Chorus in *Nabucco* when they, when they perform *Nabucco* which they couldn't, I mean they couldn't take that one off the list because that was really just normal, every opera has that on the list, but it has a very strong nationalist message, erm, so when the Slave's Chorus came the whole of the audience stood up in silence and there was this silent protest, so it was very, very, those things were very strong, and they got through to me and I suppose to my brother maybe a little bit less because he was four years younger and he left when he was 11, erm, but, but I was very, I felt very strongly about, erm, about being proudly Hungarian and later, much later on I realized how nationalist that was actually, and how much the things which, especially my father held in great esteem, er, were actually quite, maybe far, maybe not far right, but definitely right and very nationalist ideals. For example, he had this, he had, erm, these bound magazines from the 1930s, from very early 1930s when he was a kid, erm, of the Scout Movement, of the Hungarian Scout Movement, erm, and only, it took me about ten years to realize how blatantly

anti-Semitic, nationalistic right wing that movement was, and in fact the Hungarian Scouts afterwards supported the Hungarian regime's affiliation with Nazi Germany, erm, but for me at that point they were great stories because, because they were in Hungarian, they were about Hungary, they were about something that I, that I thought it was like a forbidden fruit, that we didn't have, erm, and it was the Scout Movement, which I didn't have in my childhood, we only had the Pioneers, which was the Communist equivalent, which my, my parents disdained, erm, so.

Her Hungarian identity developed alongside her mother's Jewish identity. This caused a good deal of confusion in Eva's early years at school.

So the fact that my mother was Jewish was completely, I was completely oblivious of it, erm, until I was about eight or nine, and then we had to go to school and we had to, erm, each of us had to stand up and there was some kind of census made, erm, and say what nationality our parents are and whether they are party members or not, and I very proudly stood up and I said that my parents were Hungarian and they were not party members, which I was particularly proud of, erm, and then I went home and my mum said 'What happened today at school?' and I said, 'Well, I had to say and so', and 'What did you say?', 'Well, I said that you were Hungarian, said that you were not party members' and my mum looked at my … and said 'Well, you're not actually, erm, if you ask me about my nationality I suppose that I'm not, I'm Jewish, not Hungarian'. And I thought, 'OK', so I went back next day to school and I put up my hand and I said 'I made a mistake yesterday, my mother is not Hungarian, my mother is Jewish'. And there was this silence in the class. And one of the kids from the countryside said to me, 'A real Jew?' [laughs] because she knew my mother, I don't know what they heard in the countryside about Jewish people. And she knew that my mum definitely didn't have two horns and a tail, so she couldn't believe that my mother was a real Jew [laughs]. So, and I thought, what an odd question, of course a real Jew, not knowing what that meant. So, er, so and then, then I suppose, I think the chronology may be a bit mixed, because I can't remember, but I went home one day and took down two books from my father's very big library, which I was forbidden to touch. There were only about two or three forbidden books and they were on the last shelf, and I was told not to touch them, that I would get to read them when I'm a bit more grown-up, and of course that's the worst thing you can tell a child. So, er, the moment I was, you know, big enough to climb a chair and reach them, I reached them, and they were about the holocaust, with, erm, explicit pictures of, you know, Bergen-Belsen and all that and the camps, and I was very, very shocked. I had absolutely no idea that this was, erm, that this had happened. By that time I knew that my mother was Jewish, so, I, it's it, it made me, erm, I suppose empathize with that side, er, with something that I had absolutely no idea what it was about, but because of it people were persecuted, so because we were Hungarians and we were, supposedly persecuted, erm, it pushed me to be very, to feel a great empathy and sympathy with, with that, and with the fact that my mother was, was Jewish and belonged to this, and I was very confused as to why, how come she didn't die, and how come she is alive, erm, and I had nightmares for days after, after, afterwards with this, with these pictures and the books, I think I must have been quite young, maybe ten or something, and then of course I had to confess to my parents that I'd done that and that's why I'm having nightmares and I'm having [laughs], I was really told off, but my mother did explain to me what had happened and how come that they survived, they survived because they were in Romania, not in Hungary at that time, because Transylvania at that time, in, during the Second World War went back to Hungary and all the Jews were deported, whereas she comes not from my town but from a town three hours away, which at that point was in Romania and Romanian Jews survived, so that's how they survived, erm, so that, that, that was an explanation, but still, and also because I think, erm, because my mother was a victim herself to a violent husband, then that got connected somehow in my mind, erm, so she was Jewish and she was a victim and she was a victim of her husband and her husband was Catholic, and so it was all slightly mixed.

This primal split between Hungarian and Jewish identity was accompanied by her avowedly 'very normal life' in the streets around her home.

Eva captures the texture of her everyday life as a child in Communist Romania, stressing again and again its essential 'normality', 'very, very normal … very every day, nothing, nothing special'.

Yes. Well, I think the, the, the main thing was that, erm, because of the, erm, the way, the layout of the, erm, Communist buildings when, when, when, erm, erm, in the Ceausescu era, erm, lots of peasants were urbanized because he wanted to go basically from an agricultural country to an industrialized nation, so what he did was built all this heavy industry and brought the peasants in to be workers instead of peasants and it was the most disastrous thing, but it did give, erm, er, it did give birth to all these neighbourhoods of Communist high risers, erm, and those high risers I, I grew up in one, erm, and because of the, the layout of the neighbourhood, erm, it was, er, lots of little streets with all these high risers, and lots of, you know, little green patches between them, I suppose it's like an estate would be here, erm, a council estate except even higher, higher blocks and even bigger, erm, and very, very little, erm, traffic, erm, so one of the, one of the big things was that, that we didn't grow up in the flat, we grew up out of it, you know, in the street [chuckles], in the street and in the playground, of which there were quite many, erm, kind of you know, not very fantastically equipped but nevertheless playgrounds, erm, and, and between the, between the houses, so we used to have our little street gang. Erm, and, er, a normal day would be that you were at school from eight till one or two, erm, and then you came home, in my case by bus, about you know about 20 minutes by bus, erm, then had lunch and then, erm, go out and play with the other kids in the block, erm, who were very mixed, Romanians, Hungarians, Germans all together, erm, and you would, you would do all the, the child play, child play things, erm, very much outside, very much not, erm, television was not part of it because, erm, because of the electricity shortage, of the 1970s and even then even worse in the eighties, the television, erm, the national channel only broadcast for two hours a day, from eight to ten in the evening and then on Sundays a bit more, but from eight to ten you'd have the television, erm, and we did have a set unlike some other people, erm, but all you could see was, erm, Ceausescu visiting yet another agricultural co-operative, erm, and some folklore programmes and then maybe a movie, maybe not, erm, so, television was definitely not the main attraction, and computers were non-existent [chuckles] so that was not, that was not something that you did, erm, so you were basically out, outside, erm, playing with your mates, getting on the bike, playing in the playground, you know, doing, getting up to all mischief that kids do, and, and reading, because I was a, I always read a lot, so I read through all the staple children and teenage literature of the time, and even that I didn't do inside, I would have my little hiding place where I would go outside and read my book. Erm, that was not, inside the flat was only for the morning and evening. Erm and then I would come home and practise and then do my homework and then have supper, go to bed, and that's it. So it was very, very normal, very, out of, out of house type, very communal, erm, and there was always someone who would be around to play with, erm, or if there wasn't you occupied yourself outside on your bike or, erm, and then when my brother who, he's four years younger, was old enough then we'd both go out, and we would both be part of pretty much the same gang and both tried to kill ourselves on the bike [laughs] and so it was, it was, that's why I said that it was very, very normal, very, I suppose, you know, very every day, nothing, nothing special.

But beyond the normal street life there were the tensions over ethnic identity, whether it be Hungarian or Jewish. In fact, there was also a very specialized life developing in school. For Eva went to a specialist music school, one of five in the country established by the Communist government. After talking about her normal life, she was asked if large numbers of children practised music.

No. That was something that was done in the school that I went to and the school that I went to was a, was a regional school, so there was only about five dotted around the country, so that they would have, erm, as I said before these kids coming from the countryside. Erm, but I was lucky because it was in my city, so it was, you know, half hour bus away, erm, and of course all the kids there who went music school, because it was a specialized music school, I suppose it's the equivalent of the, maybe the Purcell school and the Menuhin school here, which is up to 18 very, high powered, you know, geared towards excelling in that one thing, erm, and you would, you would have to, of course you would have to do your practice, there is no doubt about it, but that was, that was part of, it was because I always grew up with it, it was not something that I thought was very special, erm, and because my friends, not my friends from the street because I was one of maybe two, who went to that school, because my parents were musicians, erm, but, erm, certainly my class mates all did it, so it was something, just something that you did and you had to have your exams at the end of the year so, and you had to do well so, that was not, no, no question of not doing it and my mother told me much later that in the first two years she used to practise with me and I have absolutely no recollection of that whatsoever [laughs]. I always thought I practised alone but apparently not.

The music school allowed her to transcend the normal life of the street, whilst also wishing to remain vigorously part of it:

The school was absolutely wonderful and I got a lot of help so that was, that was great, and I made very quickly friends with quite a few people in the class, so, erm, so that was, that was much better, erm, I felt that that was much better socially, erm, I was better off then, than before. Erm, before I had a very select circle of friends from school, we had the gang, you know the street gang, but the street gang was you know, until the age of 12 or 13 and then we all went quickly on, when you're a teenager you don't do that any more, erm, and in my, in my school, in the, in the music school, erm, I suppose I must have been a teacher's pet [chuckles], I must have been in every, every student's nightmare, the one who always puts up her hand, and the one who always knows the, wants to know the answers and the, and the one who the teachers like, so that's not a good thing for, for your peers [laughs], not at all. So, so that must have been, it must have been a bit of a hindrance and I had absolutely no idea about it, erm, and I suppose because life at home was, was not so, not so good, erm, school was an escape, erm, and I idolized adults, I idolized my teachers, also probably because of what was going on at home, erm, and wanted very much to be liked by them. It was much more important for me to be liked by them than my peers. My peers I looked a bit down on, and, they weren't important ones who it was important for me to be liked by, erm, and when I went to Israel I understood that, you know, that was not so much like that, and also you know, because home life changed I suddenly had other, other priorities, erm, so I made good friends with, with some people in the class and we started having this very nice social thing whereby you know, erm, kids come to sleep over with you and you go to sleep over with them, and within the four years of my high school my mum had kind of an open house [chuckles], just two mattresses out almost permanently, then, and I was always going to sleep with this friend or that friend, or, and that was absolutely brilliant, that was really, that was very, very, different socially from what I knew before, so I was very, as you know two or three years later, it was absolutely wonderful.

At this time, Eva was concerned to 'excel' in her music. She was asked 'Did you always want to excel?' And she replied: 'I think as long as I remember. That's really sad [laughter]. It's true. It really is quite sad. But yes, yes. I think so. I think so.' The interview continues to explore this theme:

Interviewer: What do you think makes you, what is it that gives you that …?
Eva: That urge?
Interviewer: Urge, yes.
Eva: That's very, I don't know. Erm, I think, I think the beginnings were very much because, because of, as I said, because of what was going on at home, erm, and I needed to be liked, and I somehow made the connection that excelling will make me liked by adults. Erm, when you're, when you're a kid and when you're, you know, er, the kind of kid who, erm, erm, knows that, we have this little paper of me being in the radio programme, aged four, and they're asking me the names of the planets, because my father taught me the names of the planets and I knew the names of the planets [chuckles]. So they asked me the names of the planets and then they asked me which one was the biggest and I said that Jupiter was the biggest, and then they asked me how big did I think it was, and I said well, like, like two ten-storey buildings on top of each other, because that was the biggest thing I could imagine because my building was the biggest thing I knew [laughing], so two of those must be *non plus ultra* of how big it was. So I suppose when you're that kind of a kid, erm, then adults like you, because they like, oh, how clever, you know, that kind of very condescending, erm, atmosphere, erm, and I suppose I liked it. I liked being liked. Erm, and then I worked out that if I'm clever and if I keep being clever and I keep doing, you know, excelling and being the most this and the most that, erm, then I'll be liked, and that's why I said that it took me a long time to work out that that's not the only thing you need in life [laughs]. It took me a very long time to work that one out, which I suppose is not so clever, to, to have that, you know, to take that long to work it out. Erm, but, er, it was a very particular, it was an intellectual excelling, you know, or excelling in what you do, not excelling as a person, as a, in your qualities, but in what you know and how much of it you know.

This focus on technical learning and excellence had profound consequences for her musical career as well as her view of life and learning.

I have a very good friend who lives now in Israel who we grew up together with, in Romania, in the same class and we were best friends, and her mother was a violin teacher in the school, erm, and I didn't study with her but many of my peers did, erm, and then they came to live in Israel. And many, many, years later she heard me in a concert and then she told me that when I was little, erm, you know, about 12 or 13, I used to play, it always used to be very much in tune and with a pretty sound, but it was completely emotionless. Absolutely no expression.

The following developments cover the years of migration that followed her period in music school:

> When I was 15 my mother decided that she wanted to emigrate to Israel. Erm, Israel because it was the only possibility to get out of Romania. Erm, she could have emigrated to Germany, which would have been a lot better for her because she is a German speaker, whereas in Israel she was 50 at the time and she was, [?], but, erm, so, erm, and she's, er, been involved in opera as a pianist, in Germany there would have been a lot more, erm, possibilities for employment, given the fact that in Germany there is an opera house in every, almost in every village, whereas in Israel there was one and it was in its infancy at that point. So, erm, but because we had first degree relatives, i.e. my grandmother, who's emigrated in 1960, erm to Israel, and in Germany we only had second degree relatives, erm, the law was such that we could emigrate to Israel but not to Germany, erm, so we had to go there, and that was very much in, erm, well, a sort of economic decision, but it was more for the future of the children because my mother realized that us being Hungarians was very much hampering our chances because at that point there was always *Numerus clausus* in university intake and if you had a Hungarian surname, which I very much do, erm, then that would, that would seriously hamper the chances of higher education and careers and lives, et cetera, et cetera, and she said no, erm, that was, that was definitely not what she wanted for her children. Erm, my father decided at that point not to come, because, he said that, he wouldn't feel at home in any way, shape or form in Israel, and actually that was the second reason, which was a very personal reason, he was an alcoholic and he was a violent alcoholic, so I think that was also my mum's way of, of getting away, as he would not consent to divorce, erm, in Romania. He wouldn't hear of it. Erm, so the plan was, the master plan was that we would go to Israel, and then when my father would retire he would try to go to Germany and we would then reunite in Germany, which my mum consented to say 'yes, yes', but of course, erm, decided not to do eventually. Erm, so my father stayed behind, they divorced, my father stayed behind, erm, and my mother, me being 15 and my brother being 11, went to Israel where, as I said, well, all three of us were, erm, obviously [?] and couldn't read, write or speak, so that was an interesting year, er, interesting for me because for me it was an adventure, I think much less interesting for my mum [laughs], who was 50 years old, came out with absolute nothing, erm, obviously, erm, money was not transferable and it was, wouldn't be of any value at all, erm, so she came with what she has, with three suitcases and then some cases which came after us with, erm, books, music, and, erm, you know, personal objects, and that was it, er, and a big zero in the bank account. So, and she really, she was 50, so it's not, it wasn't an easy decision, erm, and within a year she was coach pianist in the opera class of the Tel Aviv Academy of Music, and I was in music school and my brother was in school, erm, so it was going as well as it could have gone, erm, and the next ten years I lived in Israel. Erm, the first four years were spent just in high school.

Eva describes the move to Israel at the age of 15 (her mother was 50 and her brother 11) as a huge adventure and one she was committed to. But she also speaks of her sense of escaping the dysfunctional home. The two props of her identity, the violin and her books, offer a kind of 'life raft', a sense of continuity and enduring identity, holding on to her Hungarian identity in the moment of assimilation.

> Well, I mean, I did say it was an adventure and that's exactly how it, what it felt like. At first, it didn't seem real. It didn't seem like real life. It seemed like everything was different, from, I mentioned I think before, the feeling that, the feeling of freedom, freedom of speech, freedom of thought. That was very, very, very different. Erm, but then everything else was different too. The climate was very different. It was very hot, it was a Mediterranean climate. Erm, the air was of different quality; the smells were different; the, the light was different. Er, the landscape was definitely different because where I grew up was, erm, hilly, I suppose not dissimilar to the Downs, erm, very hilly, erm, the forests and so on and Israel is in the desert, so [laughs] everything was, everything was absolutely different. There was not one thing that was the same as before except our family unit, minus my father, which was, as I said, a good thing, because he was alcoholic and it was a good thing that he stayed behind. So, in that respect it was a huge relief that, you know, the scenes that we were witnessing were, were not going to be there any more. So that was, that was one of the best things, erm, in the early, in the early days, this relief that we can get on with life without, you know, my father becoming violent and so on. Erm, and the other thing was the violin. That was, that was, that came from the old world to the new [laughs]. So, so those were the only two things, erm, and the books, the, the many books that we, that we brought with us, which of course I then began, began reading even more avidly just so that I know that I still keep my Hungarian identity and, and so on, erm. And there was this whole thing to discover, the, the world that we entering, it was all there to be, to be discovered and to be lapped up and, and, and assimilated. And I suppose, erm, the first thing that I wanted to do is to very quickly learn, learn the language, erm, and I must have learnt it quite, quite quickly because two, three months after we got there I went to school, and I remember that, that, that I was interviewed and they didn't believe that I was only three months there and that I didn't know Hebrew before and so on, and, then they sent me onto a chat show, television chat show [laughs] on prime time television [laughs], ugh, anyway, because I learnt Hebrew so, so fast.

This sense of competing identity options is clear in the choice of the violin and books as her 'old world' props. The books and the desire to keep her Hungarian identity are plainly related to her father and his political activities. She has definitely considered following in his footsteps at one stage before the alcoholism and violence disvalued such a model. She noted other models that in a sense confirmed the 'road not travelled' but admits:

> For a long time I felt when I went to Israel, for a long time I felt like a traitor, a traitor of the cause, of my Hungarian affiliations and I thought I should, I should

follow my father's footsteps and be a campaigner, et cetera, et cetera, and interestingly enough we, we knew quite a few people, erm, a university professor, lady who organized, erm, a group of students and got into huge troubles with the secret services, erm, and so on, erm, and she went completely down the hill, downhill, erm, when, erm, when the Wall fell after, after 1989, she, when suddenly everything was palpable and things were as you would have wished them but you never had, there was no struggle to be had, and her personal life fell apart, and she became an alcoholic and, et cetera, et cetera, et cetera, this is, it's a very, very, very, sad story.

And later:

When I first went to, to Israel that it was, that I was kind of maybe, maybe I was betraying the cause and I was running away, and I shouldn't do that and I, I, I should at some point go back and continue the struggle, which of course was not a struggle any more, but we didn't know that three years before the Velvet Revolution.

From this moment on, having abandoned a life of political opposition, and having left her father and Romania behind, she has nonetheless continued to search for a project that honours this search for wider meaning. These have taken the form of what she calls later her 'little crusades'. Her first phase was to embrace the Jewish religion:

I had my religious phase aged, I think about one year after I got there, because I was complete, I was very intrigued ever since that Sabbath that I described to you, erm, what it was all about, erm, and I started reading and started asking people and started discovering this fantastic wealth of, erm, what in my mind, erm, linked up with the fascination with the intellectual and I perceived it as, you know, centuries of intellectual activity, erm, and it seemed, the religious society, historically, seemed to be a society that, that did a lot of thinking and there were all these texts, the rabbinical text and the rabbinical scruples and cords and, and, and how they tried to organize everyday life, erm, and it was absolutely fascinating. So I got into, I got heavily into that and I, I had a teacher, a literature teacher, erm, who kind of adopted me, erm, and she and her husband, erm, were tutoring me in these things. And that was absolutely brilliant, erm, that was, that was, that was very, very fascinating. Er, er, very unfortunately of course I, I tried to, to do, you know, to wear skirts, erm, and long sleeved dresses, to my mother's great dismay and slight worry, erm, but then aged 17 I went to a music camp, I got a scholarship to go to a music camp in the States, and that was when, when the religious phase stopped.

She later comments on her psychological needs in the early phase of the disorienting migration to Israel, but the scrutiny of religion seems to hark back to the need for activity as an intellectual, a reader, an engaged person, someone with a degree of creativity connected to her Romanian self and her old world with its 'little hiding place' where she could retreat to read.

> It was something of being different of everyone, being very much myself, being, you know, having my own ideas and my own identity and all that, so it was, I think it was part of that, part of being an individual, erm, which then, as I said, had to be a bit toned down when I came here [laughs], because I was, I, erm, I suppose I didn't want to, yeah, I didn't want to be just one of, one of the fold, one of the many, because – and that's also probably comes from childhood because my father, you know, stuck up for minority rights and so on, erm, so I continued, that kind of, being rebellious, sticking up for something that I believed in, sticking up for something that's, that I considered were important values, to me, erm, and never mind that the rest of society that I'm functioning in doesn't, because I do so, I'm going to do it that way, erm, so I think it was part of, you know, part of, also it was, it was something that, erm, definitely the first years were, you know, were difficult years, you know, different society, erm, and it was an escape as well, it was definitely a, a psychological escape.

Her concern about injustice and oppression continued to influence her activities in Israel, where she joined peace marches and demonstrations against General Pinochet's regime in Chile – she says 'I always get involved, and that's definitely part of it, that's definitely part of, whenever I see something that I perceive as injustice, then I march in there and say, tell them what's what [laughs].'

Interviewer:	So where do you think that that comes from? Where does that sort of sense of ...?
Eva:	Erm, I think, well again, yeah, maybe I'm inclined to, to, to explain things more psychologically, but I think it comes from, well I definitely know it comes from, erm, having seen my mum as, as a victim of my father and having perceived that it's very, very unfair and very unjust, erm, and not being, not having been able to prevent it, not having been able to stop it, erm, I did try to, you know, to, to, to go and, and beat him up which was not very successful, aged 11 or 12 [laughs] wasn't so successful, but, and I did try to make him angry so that, so that he would hit me rather than my mum, erm, and I was getting really shirty and saying awful things knowing that I would provoke, er, his rage. So I did try these tactics but of course I was just a child trying, erm, and I think, I think I understood that the things that were unfair bothered me a huge, a huge amount. So then I translate that into different, different situations, and whenever I feel, I see someone threatened, erm, I boil up [chuckles], and I do, I suppose I do what, what the little kid couldn't do, which was to try and prevent it from, from happening, so I'm sure, I'm sure that in my personal case it comes from, it comes from what I saw at

home, erm. And also, erm, there was the bigger, the bigger context of, of the minority being repressed, of the Hungarians having been repressed which I thought was hugely, hugely unfair because, erm, they were preventing poets from publishing poetry and people publishing articles and plays being played and opera being performed and all that and, and it was not right, it was not, not just. Erm, so that was, that was something that, that again, that I, I think I was steeped in that kind of, erm, atmosphere where you try to state, to stand up and demonstrate against, against that, even though it's considered dangerous, in fact the more dangerous it's considered the better [laughs].

Interviewer: But again, it seems to come from the family background.

Eva: Yes. It comes definitely from the family, from the family background, on a personal level and on the, erm, immediate, immediate surroundings level, because that's what I, that's what I saw and I knew that the apartment of our, my father's very close friends with the kids with whom I grew up were searched every Thursday night, that's when they seemed to come, to, to search the whole apartment and create a huge havoc and you know, cut up the sofa and everything every Thursday night, erm, and we used to hide, to hide the books they were looking for [laughs], the forbidden books.

Interviewer: Right.

Eva: I knew exactly where they were in the flat, in our flat, they were in our flat so it was quite lucky actually that our flat never got searched, erm, but, but there was definitely that, erm, of, of being against something oppressive and I heard the stories of, you know, that, that lady who was a, university professor, she was being followed everywhere by an agent, erm, and they've both been interviewed, quite a regular basis, and, er, local officers of the local KGB. And then there was a, there was an actor who my mum and dad worked with, they worked in the opera house within the same building, there was also the theatre, and one of the actors who I knew, erm, was, erm, got drunk and peed in the middle of the night, on a statue of a great Romanian leader [chuckles] and the police got him and he was so, he was so badly beaten that both his arms were, were, erm, were broken, erm, and his face was a pulp, but, but it's his arms that I remember, I remember him being in, erm, you know two plasters. So I knew exactly why, why that was and obviously I was told, erm, so, so all those things were, were very, you know, something that you obviously spoke out against. It was just what you did, there was no other possibility [laughs]. So, so I suppose that's where the rebellious, you know, streak comes from, so then I translate it into, as I go along life I translate it into various different bits [laughs].

This extended quote summarizes the complex legacies *learned* from both the role of the mother as victim and also from the father, who for all his faults struggles against ethnic oppression in a brave and principled way. Eva's commitment to social justice, when she seeks to translate this legacy into different situations in her own life, honours the role of both parents in different ways. In seeking translation she is, it seems, feeling a way to develop an integrated identity project that provides *opportunities* for ongoing agency and learning. This search provides a huge stimulus for a variety of learning strategies.

In formulating her next crusade, Eva draws on her third definition of learning in new ways, learning to be a good person, a person with empathy and profound social relationships. Eva's new project is the promotion and performance of baroque music. Having arrived in Israel, finished high school, completed two years of army service and attended music academy, she was drawn to baroque music:

> It's a movement to, to interpret different musical styles on the instruments that that music was written for, so, to play Bach and Mozart not on the violin as we know it today but on the violin with gut strings and a different shaped bow that they would have known. And of course because there was something slightly subversive about it, and something not quite mainstream, that was hugely appealing for me. It was just like, you know, being involved in the Hungarian side when I was a youth, erm, so I got massively involved in that and that was something that is very developed in Europe but unfortunately not so developed in Israel. Erm, and I realized when I finished my studies and I worked for a year there freelancing with orchestras and doing my baroque stuff and teaching, that if I want to be a baroque musician, that will not happen in Israel exclusively because there is way, erm, so, because of I suppose you could say career choice, I decided to try and look elsewhere, and it was very much a question of, well, let's, let me see what I'm worth, out there.

This new work, she sees as a kind of crusade:

> I suppose I have, you know, I have my little crusades. Erm, for example, as I said baroque music in Israel is not so, erm, is not so, er, accepted, not so, not so much liked, erm, and I'm, I'm trying for a few years now to go back there and make a little bit of a difference in that, erm, and I can see little by little, you know, the, the people who ten years ago who have thought, you know, 'Come on, don't be so silly, what do mean, baroque music?', erm, are now coming and saying, 'Oh, actually that sounds really interesting'. People who, people who, you know, teachers, instrument teachers, instrument teachers who I knew when I was a student, erm, and who then I knew were completely against the whole, the whole idea, erm, and now if I do a lecture then you know, some people come and they say, 'Actually that was very interesting', and you know, 'Could we listen to a lesson?' and so on and so forth, so there's a little bit of a difference and that's, that's very nice. So I suppose that's my current little crusade [laughs], which is not at all a social crusade, but [laughs], but it's still something that you know that I can do to prove my point, you know, prove the point.

In these quotes we can see how she is translating her earlier political and learning dispositions into her new migrant milieu – it is slightly subversive, slightly marginal 'like being involved in the Hungarian State when I was a youth'. In this sense, it is part of an enduring identity and life project.

The social part of the project, working with other people and teaching and *persuading* them, is a central part of the crusade. This growing sense of relatedness and connectedness appeals greatly to her.

> I was personally, I was quite, erm, quite insecure in my ability to, to really make, er, make it on the level that I wanted, er, as a musician, so I was very taken up by that, erm, and the second thing was that I found society here very different from society in Israel. Israeli, Israel society is very Mediterranean, very open, erm, very talkative, very communicative, erm, on the bus you often talk to strangers, erm, just because, because you do, because there's something that, that happens that everybody starts talking about, whereas here [London], you go on the tube and everybody's buried behind the newspaper [laughs]. It's not exactly what happens, erm, even though I think, especially recent events in London showed quite a, quite a spirit of solidarity, but it only comes out in these horrible, horrible circumstances, erm, and, erm, so I, I made friends in that first year, it was a year of making acquaintances and friends, er, I made friends at the college and I made friends through, through work, erm, but I found friendships not, possibly not as meaningful as the ones that I was accustomed to in Israel, and of course now I understand that it was because, because they're formed at a different stage, and friendships formed at different stages are different kinds of friendships. Erm, I, I have absolutely wonderful colleagues, and very generous people who have, you know kind of looked out for me, erm, but I felt quite isolated in the first, in the first year, so that was a very difficult year, but it was also very exciting year on the other hand because I, because I wanted to, you know, as I said, see what I'm worth, and I was getting opportunities and chances, erm, so, so that was a, that was a good, a good thing. Erm, in the, and in the next, in the next years, erm, I think those initial friendships that I made, some of them stayed and deepened, and of course some of them just went their own way, erm, but those, those that deepened I'm, I'm very grateful for because, er, because I think when, when you come here at, at that age, erm, friendships are the best things that you can rely on, erm, and if you don't have friends you're very, very isolated, and in, in this environment especially that's, that's not a good thing, erm, so I think now I would say that I have definitely quite a few very, very good close friends, erm, and that is very lucky, I consider it very, very lucky.

She also began her first long-term relationship at this time.

> After that first year came another at least two years which were quite difficult, but then I had my first serious relationship here and I think that made a huge difference and that is a completely personal, personal thing which could happen

anywhere to anyone, erm, but that, I think that is the thing that makes to me a huge difference, is, is not being on my own struggling against the world as it were, er, but being part of a, part of a, of a couple, and, and having someone to, to, to download to in the evening, and someone who cares in the, in the way that, that a couple cares about each other, and that was, that was a very new experience and I was very, obviously because of my family history, erm, I was quite, erm, afraid, erm, of being disappointed obviously, erm, and I had a absolutely wonderful first year's boyfriend, it couldn't have been, I couldn't have been luckier, so I understood that I don't have the same thing, erm, I will not perpetuate my, you know my mother's role as a victim, er, in her relationships, er, but I can actually go some different, some different route and I think that was one of the more, more defining moments in my, in my ten years, ten years here, erm, and that relationship ended after three years.

Incrementally, Eva has developed a life project, a circle of friends, a new partner and a sense of not being alone against the world. Her life project provides a kind of answer to the question as to who she has become, and where she belongs:

It's interesting because when people ask me who, you know, what do you, erm, what do you define yourself as, the answer is always, I don't know, I don't know any more because my mother tongue and my culture which I grew up in and which I still try to keep going is Hungarian, erm, I do not use it every day. I only speak Hungarian to my mum and I read it and that's it. I do not know what's going on in Hungary, I'm not current with the, erm, literary developments, with the political developments, I don't keep any interest in that, erm, then I suppose in some ways I'm Israeli because my passport it says Israeli, that's what it says [laughs]. So if that's the defining thing then, then in some ways I'm Israeli because, because, erm, I think there is a way in which I relate to people which is you know, in a way very in line with how other Israeli people relate, so I can see, I can see that, erm, and I suppose I, in some ways I feel that I belong there inasmuch as I have lots of very good friends there and I go back almost every year, at least once if not twice, erm, for musical reasons I try to, erm, further the cause of baroque music there, so I've been invited to do some lectures and some, some classes and some, some concerts and so on, so I try to make a little bit of a difference, so maybe that's how I continue my [laughs], my life, making a difference, but it's a very small, it's a very small contribution, erm, and, erm, it's my pet, pet hobby, erm, erm, and when I'm there I feel very much that I belong to the place.

Slowly, she sees her background fading and a new sense of identity emerging. There, I am reminded of a Mary McCarthy quote on migrating away from home – that she found she could 'escape her own history and become herself' (Sage 1994).

After a while your background fades and who you are now stays, erm, and you're not regarded as someone who came from there and there and there and there, you're just regarded as you, as you who play now or you who socialize now or you who gets married or has a child or, and so on and so on, so the more you know your people the more present [chuckles] the friendship becomes, so that was, that was, that was a good, that was also a good thing, er, because I think I was at first perceived as something exotic and I didn't want to be something exotic, I just wanted to be a good violinist, that's all I wanted to be so.

Having moved to London to pursue her baroque music career, this process of becoming is clear in her answer to the question of what ethnic or national identity she feels she has:

I have real difficulty defining, defining that, and it's not, not the first time today that I was faced with that question and I had absolutely no idea. I don't know, by now I don't know, if you, and it's interesting because if you'd asked me ten years ago I would have given you a very clear-cut answer, and if you'd asked me ten years ago before that it would have been also very, very, very clear. Born in Romania but Hungarian [chuckles] and that would be the end of it. And then ten years later it would have been Jewish [laughs]. Jewish Israeli of Hungarian origin, erm, and by now it's, it's completely different, it's completely different. So [laughs] it's different, it evolves and it changes the more life, life goes on [pause]. One thing that I'm very sure of is that I'm not and I never will be British, that's, that's, that's quite clear to me, because I think you have to, you really have to be either born here or be affiliated by culture or by, or by parentage, erm, or by growing up here from a very early age, erm, with, with what the culture stands for here, and I don't mean English or Welsh or Scottish but I really mean British or Indian or, erm, British culture, erm, and that's not something that I will, that I will be, so I think not British, that's the one thing I'm sure about [laughs].

Even though she is clear she will not become British, Eva is well established as a major musical performer in London and now has a long-term boyfriend. Slowly, she is realizing that although she has developed her own career and identity project, her background nonetheless carries important influences:

Interestingly enough, erm, of course it changes from, from person to person, of course you always relate better to some people and less well to, to others, erm, but funnily enough my boyfriend's an academic [laughs] and someone who also grew up in a similar kind of milieu, so, erm, and someone who thinks about people, because his father was a psychoanalyst so he, he tends to analyse people in situations, erm, and that's a big bond between us because that's how we, we both, we both are, erm, and he's also, also big on, big on thinking, and again that's just, that just shows that's, however much you think that you're going to break the mould [laughs], there are things that you just keep on keep on doing because of how you were taught and where you come from.

Throughout her life, Eva has learnt from her social networks and relationships. She consistently refers to 'polestar figures' who have been influential in defining her identity project: the teacher 'who I absolutely idolized who was a very clever person', 'the very good friend who now lives in Israel who we grew up together with in Romania in the same class' and her favourite violin teacher.

> I went to a teacher who then taught me everything I know about, about the violin, and also about, that it's actually to, to express what you feel, which is never something that I thought was part of it. I thought that playing, playing was part of, you know, overcoming obstacles, you know, there's this technical difficulty there and then you have to get that note, and then you have to come down in that slide and then you have to, you know, the bowing is difficult there, and you know, and overcoming that is the achievement, not actually finding what the piece means and why, erm, the, the, you know, why the composer has written it that way and not some other way. And that was also something that I learned when I was, when I was in Israel and that's one of the biggest differences and it's made a huge difference to who am I today.

> *Interviewer:*   In what way has it made a difference?
> *Eva:*   I think it enabled me to, to express some kind of inner, inner voice and enabled me to, to feel that I can express my feelings, not only verbally but through, through music. Erm, and that was a, that was a very novel, a novel experience.
> *Interviewer:*   Are you aware of when that started to happen, I mean, is there a sort of event?
> *Eva:*   No. I'm not aware, I mean, it must have happened when I was in, throughout high school and throughout university, but it happened more and more when I found what I really liked doing which is baroque music actually. Erm, because it was something that was definitely mine and I, I, erm, I, erm, connected to it more than to the competitive high-powered mainstream music-making. Erm, and I was definitely becoming more and more aware of the need of the more expressive.

This quotation shows how Eva has learnt what her project can be, a project that expresses her inner voice, yet one that connects with her past aspirations in enduring ways. In expressing this inner voice in such a substantial way, Eva is tapping a rich vein of creativity. What Csíkszentmihályi calls 'flow' – a sense of timeless expression and ongoing learning (Csíkszentmihályi 1991).

Csíkszentmihályi and Beattie say that our life themes consist of the original source of psychic stress dating back to our childhood. They say a life theme 'consists of a problem or set of problems which a person wishes to solve above everything else and the means he finds to achieve solution' (Csíkszentmihályi and Beattie 1979: 48).

He argues, 'it often seems to be the case that one's occupational career choice corresponds with the chosen method for solving a central existential problem' (ibid.: 50). We can, I think, see this contention at work in Eva's choice of baroque music as a career. In their study of life histories, Csíkszentmihályi and Beattie found:

> In practically every protocol obtained from the professional group, the same pattern emerges. The child or young man is confronted by deep stress and questions that threaten his psychic survival. At some point he gets an inkling that what disturbs him is part of a more general human problem. Often this recognition occurs with dramatic suddenness. Once the connection between the personal existential problem and the wider issues is established, a method towards its solution suggests itself. The person has a lifetime's work cut out for him.
>
> (Ibid.: 57)

But in so doing, a life project has been established and a pattern of creative life work established, as in the case of Eva.

The connection between individual creation and social relations is at the heart of Eva's emergent definition of how she learns. In the following quotation, we see how she has moved from finding individual solutions and projects ('her own little hiding places') to a more sound understanding of human needs:

Interviewer: OK. And would you say at the moment that there are things, events in your life that you're learning for or from or through?

Eva: Definitely, definitely. Erm, they're mostly connected with, well, yeah, I mean, some of them are connected to my job, erm, which is a job that changes, erm, because I don't work in the same, er, with the same group of people always, being a freelance musician, I change the working environment every so often, every two weeks or maybe every few days in fact, and, erm, as I always, I keep learning about how I react in new situations, and what is it that I do well and what is it that I don't do so well, when I come across, erm, stressful situations with a group of people that I don't know very well, erm, so, that's definitely something that, that keeps, keeps going on. And then, the other thing that's, that is, that, erm, that I definitely learn from, er, is from teaching, erm, because when you teach you learn a huge amount very quickly [laughs], about who you are and why you do things, and how you do things, and you try to work out, and you learn from your students, you learn, erm, it's like a mirror, erm, you say something, it has a certain reaction and you know immediately that you've said the wrong thing because it hasn't brought on the reaction that you meant for. Erm, so that's a very immediate and very, erm, in your face learning process, especially teaching, teaching music, teaching the violin as I, as I do, so that's, that's from teaching. And then the third thing is, erm, that I, that I definitely learn from is from my relationships with, with my partner, my boyfriend, erm, because that's something that's again, erm, your reactions in certain situations are very immediate, and immediately afterwards you think, 'Oh dear, OK, and that's something that I shouldn't have done or that's something that I should have done', et cetera, et cetera, et cetera, so that, that's also a personal, kind of personal learning process. So I think at this point in my life they are more connected to the, maybe to the third thing that I've said, the personal examination, of how I, how I think I deal or how I think I should deal with, with the world and, and with my work and my personal life and so on.

Interviewer: Was there a point, though, where it sort of changed from being learning in a different way to learning on, about the more personal side?

Eva: Yes, I think there was. I think, erm, I think acquiring knowledge was very important for me in the first part, I, basically until I came here, until I came to England, erm, because I thought that that was the important thing. It was, it was, it was, er, erm, a social thing, connected with perceived success, with how I thought I should succeed in life, and I thought, well, if I amass a huge amount of knowledge, erm, you know, in, in what I do or in what I read or in what I, you know, how I, how I do things, erm, then, then that'll assure, erm, a certain outcome, which will be that I will be a successful professional or a successful person or, and then it was much later that, I was more than, more than 20, definitely more than 20, maybe 25, when I understood that actually how I was a person is more than 50 per cent of the, of the game, and it's not enough to be a, erm, brilliant at what you do if you're a bastard, so [laughs] not so, not so good, and that how, also that in my, in, in especially in England, erm, not so much I have to say in Israel, it's a very different way that, erm, working life in, in the, in, my particular domain in music works, because, erm, in England to be part of a team is considered essential, and being part of an orchestra means putting yourself, erm, to the greater good, in the service of the greater good of the sound that the whole orchestra creates and not sticking out and not, not being an, an individual, erm, whereas in Israel I think orchestras are much more, erm, erm, these condominiums of very strong individuals that all want to make their marks and of course in the, in the process create something which is, which is very good, but it's a very different way of putting yourself through as your, your personal self through. Erm, and, erm, whether you're sociable or whether you're, erm, you know, a bit of a tosser, erm, doesn't mean so much, erm, how you are as a player and how you are as a musician and how strong you are mean more over there, whereas here, more than 50 per cent I would say now, having worked here for ten years, erm, more than 50 per cent of how, how you succeed in this, in this job is, is who you are and how you

> relate to other people and whether it's pleasant to work with you or whether it's unpleasant to work with you, and of course you have to be a good professional, but apart from that you also have to be a good team, team mate, erm, and that was definitely a very steep learning curve [chuckles].

At the end of the interview sessions, I made a few field notes about Eva's portrayal, which capture some of the emergent themes that were thought to be important. Csíkszentmihályi says we expect that people have differential access to cognitive models in the culture, and that this difference affects 'the development of their life themes' (Csíkszentmihályi 1991).

Professional people such as Eva have considerable advantages in terms of access to cognitive models in the culture. Despite a disadvantaged and often dysfunctional home life, Eva's early specialization in music provides a vital social and material 'scaffolding' for her search for a life theme. In her music schools and academies, she had access to a range of role models or 'polestar figures', either her teachers (often idolized) or her peers (among whom she had a series of significant 'best friends').

Her emerging sense of herself as a baroque musician and her search for an integrating identity project should be read against this social context. As Marx has said, 'men make their own history but not in circumstances of their own choosing'. Here, we see a woman make her own history in a creative, reflexive and empathetic manner. The social context, whilst unusually disadvantaged and dysfunctional, nonetheless provides vital scaffolding for the quest in pursuit of a life theme. The definition of the patterns of learning, identity and agency must be read as collaboration between the individual self and the embedded social context. The process of becoming is then played out against a social context with the potential for belonging or transcending.

One of the key features of life stories of this sort is the sense in which they provide a 'commanding voice' as to what people do in life. One artist I interviewed even said, 'I felt imprisoned by my own creativity, cut off from the real world'. Certainly, such life storytellers do spend a great deal of time living 'in narration' and are prepared to make great sacrifices for the continuing provenance of their life narrative.

To some extent, then, an elaborated narrative provides a stimulating and life-enhancing life theme but, as with all things, there are downsides and the all-encompassing life theme can sometimes be experienced as tyrannous and imprisoning.

This portrayal points up the complexity of narrativity – both in its uniqueness and in its generalizable characteristics. This is an elaborative portrayal and helped in the definition of elaborated narratives explained in Part 2. Combining the analysis of interview transcripts from a variety of projects and the subsequent development of a range of portrayals, the next four chapters seek to define the major kinds of narrativity evidenced in the research. In the final chapters, the significance of these narrative styles is assessed and analysed.

Part 2

On Forms of Narrativity

Chapter 6

Studying storylines

In earlier chapters, we saw how studying people's life stories might allow us to understand different styles of narrativity – different ways of telling, living and representing our life stories. We added the important caveat that life stories themselves as a genre are specific to particular historical periods and cultural contexts. We said that focussing on life stories would possibly allow us to scrutinize some of the strategies by which people respond in different ways to life experiences and changing circumstances. Types of stories might then be part of the complex DNA of personal responses to situations. If this is true, then our life story is a lot more than just a story – it might hold a series of crucial clues as to how we act and live. It might help us to understand differences in personal styles, religious beliefs, political affiliations, community allegiances and domestic arrangements. Life stories, then, are a crucial ingredient in what makes us human and, in turn, what kind of human they make us.

Our life stories provide us with a stock of *narrative capital*: an armoury of narrative resources with which we not only render accounts but flexibly respond to the transitions and critical events which comprise our lives and equip us to actively develop courses of action and learning strategies.

Surely, though, you might say the classification and differentiation of life stories is just too big a task – are there not as many stories as there are people? Our stories must be unique and idiosyncratic and therefore well beyond any systematic understanding. The answer to this is both 'yes' and resoundingly 'no'. It is true that each of us and each of our stories is unique – just as in physical terms each of us has a unique DNA. However, we also fall into identifiable categories not only in our physical make-up but also in our type of life story.

Christopher Booker makes this point very clearly in his magisterial study of stories. He argues that in fact there are only a small number of basic storylines or plots – he says there are only 'seven basic plots' in our life story constructions. He illustrates that these basic plots cover different cultural milieux and different historical periods. They represent for him timeless archetypes which provide foundational plot lines for embellishment at the cultural and personal level. Far from being impossibly variegated, our life stories seem to cluster into a small number of 'archetypical plots' (Booker 2006).

I first began to think about the fundamental differences in narrative character as a result of an interview with the playwright Arthur Miller. Miller was heavily involved with the Arthur Miller Centre for American Studies at the University of East Anglia where I was a professor during the years 1996–2004. Much of his dramatic work has a deep narrative intensity, and so when he talked about old age it was with a depth of understanding about life stories. In answer to the question, 'What is it like to be in your late eighties?' he gave a concise answer which I can only quote from memory (the interview was not recorded):

AM:	I think many of my generation have a fairly similar experience – they watch a lot of daytime TV and they spend a lot of time dozing …
Interviewer:	What about you?
AM:	[Long pause] I tend to get up fairly early and I work away thinking and writing. I break for lunch with my wife … then I am back at it till the early evening.
Interviewer:	So you are very different to a lot of your generation?
AM:	I guess so.
Interviewer:	Why do you think that is?
AM:	[Long pause] Well you know I think it is because … because … I am the kind of person who is constantly in the process of becoming as I develop my story …

This conversation of Miller's was so generative for me because it pinpointed the importance of variegations or differentiations in narrative constructions as well as personal orientations. His generation's experience of old age for the great majority followed the conventional script of old age – partly daytime television and a comfy armchair – but because of his history of narrative becoming, Miller's experience was utterly different. Of course, these differences involve a range of other factors beyond narrativity – health being an obvious one – but they point up how a narrative trajectory and a habit of 'becomingness' can support a very different experience of old age.

My mother was a very instructive model of becomingness, and I no doubt learnt a good deal from her about this particular narrative trajectory. Sadly, she has recently died at the age of 104 and many of the stories she has told to me have come back to me as I have written this book. One particular story provides an example of the points that Miller is making. When she was 99, my mum was invited to a poetry session. Since she lost my dad at 75, she had started to write poetry and this is how she tended to define herself, I realized. She saw herself as a poet. This was a very strongly held image and grew out of her frustration as a highly intelligent woman who had had to leave school early to work in a factory.

The problem with the life vision she developed in her later years was that her poetry was of a fairly basic sort: pretty much in 'the cat sat on the mat' kind of category, it has to be admitted. The problem culminated in the weeks after her

99th birthday, when she phoned me up to tell me how things were going. I can recall the conversation fairly clearly:

> I've got a really interesting weekend, me duck. I am going to a poetry gathering in Torquay. They have a poet in residence and they are all going to gather round and give our poems and I'll see how it goes.

The following weekend I went down to Devon to see my mum and asked, 'How did the poetry weekend go?' She said:

> It wasn't good, duck. It wasn't good. They all gave their poems – very elaborate poems – all sorts of complicated things that didn't rhyme properly. Then I gave my poem and there was a terrible silence at the end bit. Nobody said anything. And then you wouldn't believe it, they invited all the people to come to the next poetry symposium and they didn't mention me.

This dénouement did leave me worrying how to soften the blow for my mum with regard to her sense of identity and aspiration. I decided probably the best way was to meet the issue head on and I said, 'Mum, I think it is just possible that you are not going to make it as a poet.' I said it half in jest and half seriously so she could take it either way. She looked at me very sadly and there was a long pause and she said, with a voice of utter wistfulness and regret, 'Yeah, you could be right.' At this point, I realized that my 99-year-old mum was very much in the process of aspiring and becoming, and that her narrative was precisely of the sort that Miller's exemplifies. She was still writing her poetry and publicly giving renditions of versions right up to the end of her life, and even at 104 was actively pursuing her vision of poetry as a vocation. The poetry is only part of the question of understanding my mum's identity project. I believe she was actively working on her narrative, and that in spite of its problems it provided her with great vitality and a central spine of aspiration at a time when other people were residing in comfy chairs in front of the daytime television that Miller talks about.

The Miller interview echoes the tone of Jean Paul Sartre's ruminations on selfhood, but even more the wonderful study of 'Old Age' by Simone de Beauvoir with the generative first line, 'One is not born a woman but rather becomes a woman,' and her insistence that 'life consists of going beyond oneself' (de Beauvoir 1972).

It would seem that some people are indeed driven to go beyond their birthright script and are driven, in the process of becoming to which Miller eludes, to construct a distinctive sense of self through narrative construction. In her recent book, *Crazy Age*, Jane Miller gives us a number of glimpses of this process of narrative construction. She argues, rather reluctantly, that in her experience, and the book is about her experience of old age,

> There does seem to be a kind of will in us, there from birth, which directs us and holds us together and starts us on the road to distinguishing ourselves decisively from the people around us.
>
> (Miller 2010: 192)

Helen Small talks of how people's narrative capacity is eroded by old age. What we see as conventional old age, then, may be as much about narrative decline as an organic deterioration. This might help us to understand the points that de Beauvoir and Arthur Miller are making. As Small says in *The Long Life*: 'With narrative we must be canny, or we shall find ourselves overwhelmed by the onward rush of chronology' (Small 2007: 112).

In old age, the variations in narrative capacity are as wide and comprehensive as the other variables of human existence; in old age, these inequalities of capacity and resources are actually exacerbated. Narrative capacity can certainly erode with age and Small argues this may be a benign development for some but not for others:

> If there is a severe loss of capacity we may do better to reject the narrative view altogether. That is, we may find it kinder and more in keeping with the person's ability to give shape to their own life. To place less emphasis on narrative preserving it only weakly, as a dotted line to indicate the fact of an ongoing life. In less extreme cases, we may leave considerable room for variation in people's sense of whether the narrative view is a positive resource enabling them to think of their lives or the lives of others in terms of meaningful continuities and formal integrity, or whether it becomes, after a certain point oppressive – so that we do better to give the narrative view a less prominent part in our thinking.
> (Small 2007: 104–105)

Certainly, Frank Kermode sees the later stages of life in narrative terms as a 'search for intelligible endings' (Kermode 1967).

Macintyre, meanwhile, sees that 'unity of narrative' as a culminating phase in the search for meaning:

> The unity of life is the unity of a narrative quest. Quests sometimes fail, are frustrated, abandoned or dissipated into distractions; and human lives may in all these ways also fail. But the only criteria for success or failure in a human life as a whole are the criteria of success or failure in a narrated or to-be-narrated quest.
> (Macintyre 1981: 218–219)

For some people, this is the case and for others it is not. As a contemporary of mine recently commented, 'I feel my identity is in complete free fall' as 'I lose control of my life story'. If some of the stark differences, in identity projects and life stories like so many other differences, are highlighted in old age it is nonetheless true that a spectrum of kinds of narrativity can be discerned much earlier in life.

In a more general sense, life stories cluster into a number of main categories. From the beginning of my research studies in the 1980s, it became clear that there was a broad spectrum of life stories. One large section of life stories were 'descriptive', an often chronological series of factual, retrospective descriptions of what has happened to the person. In a series of interviews, the person would often repeat similar episodes or add in new descriptions of other episodes. However, the stories were described yet seldom analysed and, in the act of narration, reflection and reappraisal seldom happened. It was as if little sustained 'interior conversation' had taken place about life events – things had happened and these happenings were described. There was an essentialized, often contented, sense of 'this is what I do, this is who I am' – 'I am a farmer, I'll die a farmer, it's what I do.' A socially constructed script then provides the overriding key to the life story.

At the other end of the spectrum are life stories that involved considerable experimentation and self-construction. Here, the script seems to be heavily 'worked on' by the person, what I have called 'elaboration'. This could be clearly seen in the interviews where people elaborated and theorized aspects of their lives. It seems much more 'a work in process', and in narrating their lives the interviewer can see stories and events being 'worked upon', analysed and reflected upon and sometimes repositioned in the overall life story. Here, we got a sense of an ongoing 'interior conversation' taking place which could often be observed at work as the life story was narrated. We came to view this group as life story theorizers or more generally 'elaborators'.

So the initial spectrum for identifying types of life story was fairly simple (and as such bipolar too). It covered description through to elaboration as types of life story development (Figure 6.1).

This is of course a simplistic starting point for analysing our life stories, but it reflects my research beginnings in coming to understand how life stories can differ in basic ways. Some of the work in identifying the spectrum from scripted describers to elaborators grew out of the studies of professionals at work. In the Spencer study mentioned earlier, we could observe how some teachers followed the new government guidelines – the new script if you will – fairly compliantly, whilst other teachers – often judged as being very creative – found the script was hostile to their own elaborated professional identity. These crucial differences of response led us back to analysing how crucially different life stories and different narrative characters led to sharply different responses to new professional scripts.

By starting in this way, we began to develop a series of strategies for studying life stories so as to understand their basic differences, which we then employed in the Learning Lives project and subsequent other projects.

One strategy for characterizing our life stories is to use the concept that I call 'narrative intensity'. In our early interviews with people about their life stories, they were encouraged to tell their story with as little intervention from the interviewer as possible. We wanted, at one level, to study their narrative propensity – the degree to which they had already practised their narrative. In general, descriptive life story-tellers spoke for shorter, less intense periods and required more interviewee prompts.

Description   Elaboration

Figure 6.1 Life story development

The more descriptive life stories often covered only a few lines before an interviewer prompt was required. John Peel, for instance, spoke in relatively short snatches and in a break in the interview complained that he didn't really understand the rules for this 'false conversation'. More elaborative life storytellers spoke for long periods – in one case for more than 44 pages non-stop.

But it turned out that narrative intensity did not always equate with elaborative ways of storying. Moreover, elaboration itself was not a guarantee of effective reflectivity. The major factor in this regard proved to be not the intensity of the narration but the degree to which personal elaboration or description was linked to the development of a 'course of action'.

As an example of the spectrum of narrativity, we can see in the following diagram (Figure 6.2) how 25 life storytellers in the Learning Lives project at Brighton began

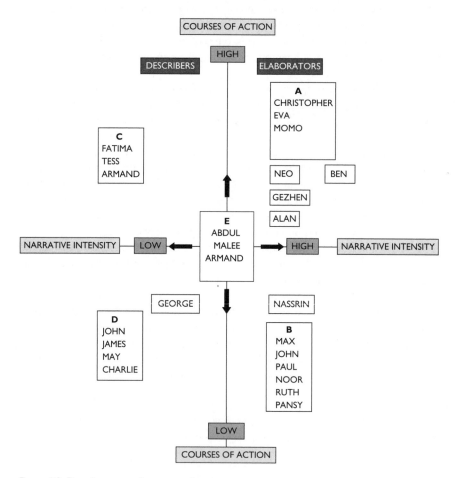

Figure 6.2 Development of courses of action

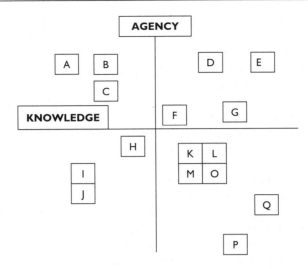

Figure 6.3 Narrativity, agency and knowledge

to cluster into groups. We locate our group of life story describers on the left and the elaborators on the right; then the spectrum of narrative intensity is plotted against the development in the life stories of 'courses of action' or an 'action focus'.

Fascinatingly, this pattern of clustering was replicated in another research initiative seeking to map knowledge and learning against patterns of personal action and agency. The mapping produces the configuration shown in Figure 6.3 (the original names have been replaced by letters).

Both of these patterns of clusters pinpoint the same issue: that narrativity and knowledge are not uniformly related to agency and action. The implications of this are substantial and question the emergence of a hierarchy of narrativity along the lines that Maslow once presented in his 'hierarchy of needs'.

Any simple conclusion that a spectrum from description at a lower end to elaboration at a higher end exists is therefore questioned. The characterization of narrativity is more complicated than any linear spectrum can portray.

As is now well known, Maslow's hierarchy of needs distinguished what he called 'lower needs' and 'higher needs'. He argued that physiological needs were the strongest and most potent – the need for food, water and sex are primary physiological needs. He states that physiological needs 'are stronger than safety needs, which are stronger than love needs, which are in turn stronger than the esteem needs, which are stronger than the idiosyncratic needs we have called the need for self-actualisation' (Maslow 1954: 57).

In a similarly binary model, Basil Bernstein argued that people's linguistic codes followed a spectrum from restricted code to elaborated code. The restricted code was local, de-contextualized and specific. The elaborated code was more theorized, abstract and contextualized, and gave access to wider understanding. It was widely interpreted as a hierarchy of competences, although Bernstein himself warned against such an interpretation.

Bernstein, however, does comment in his later work on the capacity of elaborated codes not just to develop theorized visions of life but to open up our thinking in a more fundamental way than is possible with restricted codes. He says: 'Elaborated codes are the media for thinking the unthinkable, the impossible, because the meanings to which they give rise go beyond local space, time, contexts and are embedded and relate the latter to transcendental space, time and context' (Bernstein, in Richardson 1986: 209).

Our analysis of narrativity leads to a more complex patterning with regard to scriptedness and elaboration, particularly around issues of agency and the delineation of courses of action. It remains true that there is a spectrum of narrativity from scripted describers through to more personalized elaborators. It is not true that this allows us to develop a hierarchy of narrativity along these lines. This is because narrativity needs to be linked to identity, learning and agency if we are to understand its complex social significance.

What our mapping of narrativity indicates is that those following a more descriptive mode can be as agentic and as purposeful in their learning and identity projects as those with more elaborated styles of narrativity. Both modes have action potential, identity potential and learning potential, and it is through the analysis of these potentialities rather than the characterization of narratives as descriptive or elaborative that we come to understand these complex social significances (see Goodson *et al.* 2010).

By examining storylines along a spectrum from description to elaboration, we are only at the beginning of our investigation. The binary proposition leads not to a definition of hierarchies but to an understanding of complexity. Maslow's analysis of needs, for instance, leads to a clear hierarchy of needs. Bernstein warned against hierarchy, but many of the interpretations of restricted and elaborated codes drew up hierarchical interpretations. The spectrum of narrativity from description to elaboration is no such hierarchical matrix.

This is because narratives need to be investigated not only for textual and even literary sophistication but also for their potential in the world of human action and activity. Once we examine a narrative's learning potential, action potential and identity potential, a much more complex picture emerges. The capacity to describe or elaborate needs to be specifically related to the capacity to delineate courses of action in the material world, and the relevance for learning and for developing our identity projects can be discerned within this complex conundrum.

Examining storylines does not, or should not, start then from an assumption that our capacity to narrate our lives is the key to human agency, learning or the pursuit of wellbeing and happiness. Nor should it begin from the assumption that we all narrate our lives in any systematic and sustained way. As we shall see in the next chapters, not all people are practised narrators, who reflect upon and refine their life narratives. For some, a far more descriptive account, a more stuttering storyline emerges, and for some the notion of storyline itself may overstate the kind of account they are working with.

It is, then, not only in cultural and economic terms that monolithic assumptions about narrativity must be questioned, but also in terms of each person's narrative character. This is true even when people live amongst an Anglo-American cultural milieu which stresses the dominance of individual narrative forms.

In Chapter 5, I deliberately presented a detailed portrayal in an early stage of development. This had a dual intention: to display the texture and detail of life narrative interview data and to show how thematic insights develop in a painstaking yet provisional manner. We can see in this portrayal how tentatively some understanding of the nature of what I call narrative 'elaboration' emerges.

To provide such a detailed portrayal in the process of development is important for another reason. In the following chapters on narrativity, a very abbreviated coverage of individual narratives is employed to exemplify types of narrativity. By providing Eva's portrayal in almost its entirety, the reader is shown just how detailed are the background data on which the abbreviated definitions of narrative types are based. In a book such as this, which seeks to provide a summary analysis of narrative types, one is caught between a number of potential styles of presentation. In Eva's portrayal, one can see the rich texture and detail available in the life history data, but the overarching themes can be subsumed by the personal fascination of the narrative. I have chosen in the following chapters a much more succinct style of presentation, but by presenting a full portrayal I hope to have shown just how many substantial details and data underpin these summary analyses. The development of a series of portrayals helps to form and refine the themes which are captured in the primary data.

Portrayals, then, are an interim stage between raw interview data and the rather summary conclusions that follow. For readers seeking more portrayal detail, a number of earlier books carry some of the detailed portrayals on which the following conclusions are based (in particular: a report from the Spencer project, Goodson and Hargreaves 2003; and Goodson et al. 2010). The primary data from these projects are also stored in the archives at the Education Research Centre in Brighton.

The archives from which the following narrative types are derived comprise a range of categories. For a start, there is an enormous range of primary sources in the shape of interview transcripts and field notes. Some of the characteristics of these data can be seen in the Eva portrayal. But there are also more detailed case studies of people, together with charts of their origins and destinations, characteristics and trajectories. There are charts of particular classifications and categories. There are some diaries, journals, photographs and documents.

We slowly built up a picture of different narrative types using all of these data from a wide range of research settings, and of course by engaging in ongoing conversations and collaborations with the various research teams involved.

In the following chapter I have quite deliberately sought to move beyond the detail of all the archives on which the narrative types are based. The next four chapters seek to conceptualize in short and summary form the main types of narrativity that have been discerned in these research studies. Moving from an original binary of scripted descriptions and personal elaborations, a more complex pattern emerges. The degree of scripting or elaboration is just one matrix of differentiation. Equally important is the degree of agency discerned – the capacity to delineate courses of action is another crucial axis. We then see 'scripted describers' (but also 'multiple describers'), and we also see 'focussed elaborators' (but also what we call 'armchair elaborators').

By scrutinizing the life narratives collected in the range of projects described, a number of different foci of investigation have been utilized. First, the narratives have been examined for their 'narrative intensity' and narrative quality. This is where the original distinction between scripted narratives and more elaborated narratives emerged.

When, as a researcher, you read through the transcripts of an interview these differences in the character of narration become very clear. Some narratives are fairly short and descriptive, they often embrace a clear societal role, for example, farmer, househusband or nurse, and relate this socially sanctioned and provided script with some fidelity. Others provide a narrative which has obviously involved a great deal of personal narrative work – often the speaking goes on at great length without much prompting from the interviewer. Whilst 'scripts' available in society are employed in places, the elaborated narrative is a 'personal collage', fitting together in a painstaking way a narrative that suits the individuality and idiosyncrasies of the person.

In all kinds of narratives, we begin to see different potentialities both for learning, agency and identity production. Hence, our second line of investigation is the potential for what I have called 'the delineation of courses of action'. In what sense, then, does the life narrative provide resources and indeed guidance for the way people act in the world? My sense is that for some people their narrative is a kind of 'commanding voice' not only in the way they present their life but also in the way they make key decisions – instrumental, economic, political and moral – about how to live. In other words, their life narrative is a major source of inspiration for the way they act in the world; it informs and guides their actions.

Here the kind of narrative character, its intensity and quality, provides a spectrum of differentiation with regard to the delineation of courses of action. It is at this point in any investigation of the potentialities of life narratives that any simple binary spectrum breaks down. For although scripted narratives may seem less efficacious in terms of narrative intensity and quality, their capacity for action is not necessarily different to that of more elaborated modes. At all times what is crucial is the individual question of how the narrative is *employed* in living and directing a life.

Hence, whilst for some a script provides a *closed*, somewhat pre-determined and foreclosed quality, for others scripts (in the plural) can provide the basis for a life of mobility and transformation. It depends on how the narrative is employed, and for some a script can provide a starting point and a lynchpin in a life of vigorous activity and change; it can be employed, then, in an *open* manner.

To understand how a narrative is employed, there are a number of different investigative foci that can be utilized. In my work (partly opportunistically because of the research funding available), I have focussed on the question of learning. This, though, is a crucial point to investigate how narratives are employed. It is at this point that the distinction between a *closed* use of narratives and an *open* use emerges. As we have argued in our book (Goodson *et al.* 2010), narrative learning is 'not solely learning *from the narrative*, it is also learning that goes on *in the act of narration* and in the ongoing construction of the life story' (Goodson *et al.* 2010: 127).

In this manner the life narrative is a site for learning, and in examining life narratives we can begin to see how they are employed and implicated in the way people learn. We can then assess if life narratives are working in a closed or open manner. I refer to this variable as the 'narrative capital' of a person – that capacity to deploy and employ their narrative in the delineation and promotion of courses of action and further development of learning strategies and skills.

As we shall see in the next chapters, these questions of narrative quality, the delineation of courses of action, and the development of learning strategies and skills do point up different routes and trajectories that are more or less open or closed. We shall argue that this set of dispositions is a crucial part of understanding the 'DNA of personal response' to life events and decisions.

In later chapters, we shall see how a person's narrative capital provides vital mechanisms for dealing with transitions and critical incidents, particularly in the fast-changing, flexible economies of the contemporary world.

Chapter 7

Scripted describers

In Chapter 6 we developed an initial spectrum of kinds of narrative character covering forms of descriptive narrative through to more elaborative forms. We showed earlier, however, that these narrative forms needed to be related to how people became agentic in delineating courses of action and learning strategies to use in their lives. In the next four chapters, we review the four major narrative types discerned across a range of research projects.

One of the most common forms of life stories we encountered in our research over the last decade is what I have called scripted describers. As we have seen earlier, all life stories employ, to a degree, scripts and storylines that are 'out there' in the cultural setting. Whilst we talk of self-made men and women and people who invent themselves, this is seldom done without some recourse to existing storylines. John le Carré, for instance, has commented in a number of interviews that, given the loss of his mother at six and an absent father: 'Since nobody else was there to follow I had to invent myself.' However, this overestimates the capacity for self-invention – much of le Carré's life still follows a recognizable set of storylines that already exist in the culture. As we saw earlier, many politicians regard themselves as 'self-creationists' – Obama being the most recent in a long line.

In later chapters, we will scrutinize this more personal assembling of a storyline. This invention and elaboration turns on the way in which a unique collage or jigsaw is constructed. The pieces of the jigsaw might be colonized from existing cultural storylines, but some new pieces may indeed be invented. Overall, the jigsaw picture that emerges is therefore individually conceptualized and constructed. In this chapter, we concentrate on the narratives of scripted describers.

May and John: scripted describers

Unlike those who personally conceptualize and construct parts of their life story, in the case of scripted describers there is little such work undertaken on construction or invention. The descriptive mode implies a somewhat passive recounting of what is accepted and lived. Often, the script is treated as almost a birthright. In the examples of John and May, we can see that early on in life an identity is embraced that is partially 'given' by their origins and background. In neither case do they seek to move beyond the given script in living their life. Moreover, in neither case is there much evidence of an internal conversation being conducted that might provide some reflective distance on the partially inherited script. Indeed, John is not even confident that he has a 'story' for his life. It is something that happened to him, and only very late in his life does he retrospectively wonder about other ways he might have lived his life.

May Taylor was in her late 20s and early 30s at the time of her interviews. Given the substantial news coverage of traveller sites recently, it is a significant factor that she lived on an unauthorized traveller site in Southern England. Whilst she now resides in 'the South', she was actually born and spent the formative years of her childhood in the North of England – although these were nomadic years with summers normally spent in Wales.

From early on in her life, and certainly by the end of her primary school years, she felt strongly that she was stigmatized and indeed victimized because she was a 'gypsy'. She herself accepts and articulates a strong identification as 'a gypsy'. She is fearful, even 'scared', of settling in one place and living in a house, and embraces the gypsy belief in freedom and life in a caravan.

John Peel was in his late 70s during the interviews. He was born and still lived in a small hamlet in a rural area in the South of England close to the South coast. His family were tenant farmers – farming a mixed farm on a pattern of tenancy based on personal 'gentlemen's agreements'. His father rented the farmhouse and in due course John took over this agreement when his father died in 1980. John, who died at the end of the project period, had three sons and a daughter. One of these sons has subsequently taken over the farm. John continued to work right up until the end of his life and spent his last weeks, even though suffering from terminal cancer, helping his son oversee his farm.

By using the term 'scripted describer' to characterize certain life stories, we are stressing descriptive life stories that do not move away from the original script, almost the birthright script. May sees herself as a 'gypsy woman'. John says of his parents, 'they always knew I was going farming and I always knew I was going farming', and of his life in farming, 'it was something I sort of did. My life was really in the country and getting back farming that really, to me, was life.' This is a very succinct description of a life lived in the continuing embrace of a script that was accepted early on in a life – as we said, it is almost a script as a birthright, something accepted as a sort of predestination. This kind of narrative is undoubtedly common throughout the world and far more recognizable outside the 'West', where more individualized and personalized visions emerge.

The scriptedness of description and the absence of elaboration can be evidenced by studying the narrative intensity of the life story interviews. John experiences considerable difficulty in assembling his life story for the interviewer and complains that it is a sort of 'false' creation to assemble a chronological account for a stranger. He interprets the task as chronological, but most significantly, given the tone of pre-destination in his embrace of the role of farmer, he never moves much beyond his mid-twenties in his life chronology. In describing and recounting his life story in a sense, by then the script has been settled and the role of life repeats the essential rhythms and seasons of a farmer's life. The only later event systematically referred to is when external events bring an end to his farming life.

By letting John recount his own life in his own way, particularly in our use of the 'vow of silence' for the early interviews, we can begin to see how the initial script influences his whole life. The notion that the life story involves an early narrative closure, that is, that the range of choices as to how to live and story a life is *closed* at an early stage, seems to fit with the way that John recounts his life and also the way he lives that life.

In May's case, the difficulty of telling a life story is illustrated by the short rendition she provides in the interview. This truncated account seems to reflect not just an absence of opportunities to rehearse her story, but also an absence of an ongoing internal conversation about that life story:

> Like I say, I was born in [northern city], um, I lived at [town] for a good part of me life, er, in a little village called [village] and, er, lived on a caravan site there. I went to school but I only went for six years of me schooling, that's all I had because, like, them days, like, if you went to the, the big school there was a lot of drugs, and, like, things like that in school where, travelling people doesn't like, they don't like it, so they wouldn't send their children to the secondary school, so that was all the schooling I had ... really is, from being age of four to 11, but I seem to be, like, getting on alright, like, I can read, write and do things like that, like, I'm not stuck on anything like that, um, trying to think um [pause] help me somebody, pardon?

She attributes her lack of internal and external conversations to her early experience:

> It always stuck in your brain that you was bullied, that made me very timid with people. That's why I can't talk properly [laughs]. I don't know what to say.

What both John and May seem to illustrate is that for whatever reason, a busy farming day or a different social location, little narrative work has been undertaken by either of them on life storying. Stories are told fragmentarily and no overarching narrative of life's meaning and direction has emerged. Life is busy and demanding and internal narration does not often take place in this workaday context. In such work and life situations, there is little time for internal reflection. A narrative or script is embraced early and followed with little deviation. Narrative closure is in that sense accepted early on and improvisation and change are closed off. The narrative and the way the life is acted out and lived reciprocally work to *close off* choice and alter destinations.

The context of life is stable in both cases. John was born in 1927 in a small farming hamlet and lived there until 1995 when the farm had to be sold. Throughout these almost 70 years, he says there was no real reason for going anywhere. This was, as he says, because he had no great curiosity about other prospects: 'farming and country I didn't realize there was anything else when I left school. It was only farming I wanted to do [pause]. Yes, that's all I even thought of … life was really just farming.' May learnt acceptance of the given script in a similar manner:

> Like, through the day, like, we'd get up in the morning, like, girls, like, travelling girls they'd get up in the morning, they'd, like, cook and clean for the mothers, like, wash the caravans down, like, if there was younger children but obviously I had never had no younger sisters so I used to cook, clean, make beds, wash, that's, what we used to do, like, that's what young travelling girls are supposed to do. Do you get me meaning? That's what we used to do so.

It was a deliberate pattern of socialization in a 'travelling girl' script that was learnt off by heart.

Interviewer: Did you like that?
May: It learnt us in one way that that was meant to be learned, what to do, like, so when we got a family we'd know how to cook, clean, like, make beds, wash, everything would be, like, you know what we've, be able to do it in other words where the boys would go with the fathers, and they'd learn off the fathers what to do. Do you get my meaning?

Whilst a script may be socially given and personally accepted, and whilst internal narration might be minimal, this does not mean an absence of passion, purpose and motivation. Far from it. When the script is working well life may feel acceptable or, certainly in John's case, highly fulfilling. Both have strategies for improvement. In May's case, this is displaced to the next generation of her sons:

> I'd like 'em to go to school, educate, be educated and get a good job, like, like say anything like a doctor. I get – nothing would more please me than my [name] growing up and being a doctor. Like proper, a proper living in other words, like, you know. And a salary coming in every week, where we're scrimping and saving, scraping all over, that's what I'd like for me two boys, I would. I think gypsy life's terrible. It is. Terrible I think it is … I don't think gypsy life's much good. I'd rather my sons to have a better life than that. Like, we try not to do without things, where I have had to do without things.

Scriptedness does not mean an absence of agency or development. John works hard to develop his farm and constantly looks for ways to improve matters:

> It always just seemed a natural progression to sort of try and improve and improve the farms, improve the cattle, improve, you know, the land, cattle, where the men lived and, how things changed, sort of modern machinery and we were always aiming to improve and get better …. Many other things along the way, changing times, but really it was just sort of circumstances, predicted what we did and just trying to expand all the time and get bigger, and better.

The downside of scriptedness is that it places limitations on personal agency and learning. Learning tends to be directed by the inherited scripts and as such tends to be largely instrumental learning. May's words echo the fatalism of the scripted describer. She is a gypsy woman and she's faithful to the script but she repeats: 'I think gypsy life's terrible. It is. Terrible I think it is ... I don't think gypsy life's much good. I'd rather my sons have a better life than that.'

In a sense John endures a similar fate, although he views his occupational choice much more optimistically. Growing up in the valley in the 1930s, so much of farming was based on tight community relationships of trust and honour. Business was done 'by a shake of the hand' and gentlemen's agreements were paramount. Whilst this social arrangement was in place John's script worked fine. He knew the place, the community knew him and he knew them and decisions were taken within this group. But more and more, and with increasing speed, agriculture became a market economy. He was a tenant farmer and as long as gentlemen's agreements stood he was fine, but in a market economy landlords and their hard-driving and sometimes duplicitous agents pushed the bottom line of profits and charges. After a series of reverses, crises with foot and mouth and BSE, John had to sell up and leave his beloved farm. For him, the worst part was selling his carefully tended cows:

> We got the cattle in on the, before the day before the sale, because the sale day they obviously weren't milked, because you sort of just leave them, you know, that morning don't milk them, but the day before it, think it took me sort of, well, I just stood with the cows, sort of in the morning, just couldn't let them in. But I was on my own and so nobody saw me. But as I say it still makes me feel quite, very emotional, I'm afraid. Yes, yep, very emotional.
>
> Although I helped get ready for the sale, I never went out [coughs] on the sale day, I just left it to my sons. People came, they were all sold on the farm, but I didn't go out, I kept out of the way.

And even when the farmhouse and the herd were gone, John went on working until a few days short of 80 when he died. His last journey was being driven round the old farm by his wife in the Land Rover. He has six grandsons: 'at the moment I can't see grandsons wanting to carry on farming, they all seem to have other ideas'.

At the end, we wondered, had John thought of other ways he might have lived and storied his life?

> I wish I'd, I'd come back to being intellectual there, um, perhaps I wish I'd, I, I would study more now if I was a young person, you know, I just lived to go farming, but I think now [pause], if I had my time now I think I would sort of try and learn more and, on the science, perhaps, side of it, the farming ... I don't mean I'm envious of this granddaughter now but I mean she's doing research for DEFRA and she travels ... I mean she's only 22 or 23, she's got her degree and sort of got a very good job with DEFRA, and you know doing some research on calves so she has to go round various farms which she had to find in the West

Country and she was told she should join some research thing up in Scotland ... And she's just had three or four days up ... she had to sort of take her papers and explain to them all that she was doing up there. She's going off out to Spain to, something with her papers there. And I admire her and I, you know, I wish perhaps I'd had the brains to do something like that.

In his study of why we tell stories, Christopher Booker stresses that we are all to some extent scripted but manipulate available scripts differently.

Without in any way wishing to detract from the genres of original storytellers if there is one thing emerging from the past few hundred pages it is the extent to which stories told by even the greatest of men are not their own. Their skill lies in the power with which they manage to find outward clothing in which to dress up a theme which is already latent not only in their own minds but in those of their audience.

(Booker 2006: 543)

To some extent, then, we are all working with scripts generated elsewhere. All narratives are to that extent scripted. But the degree of improvisation, and the degree of bricolage, varies enormously. A jazz musician may be playing 'Stormy Weather' but that may be the sole aspect of the scriptedness because the jazz musician embellishes and improvises the baseline script by putting her or his own personal stamp and signature on the way the time is constructed or performed. The point is the degree of improvisation which opens up the script and makes something personal and original in the process. In the genre of scripted describers such improvisations are largely absent, and hence personal construction is kept to a minimum.

People whose main mode is description tend to recount their lives as a series of things that happened to them as: 'farmers', 'housewives', 'gypsies', 'bankers', 'teachers', or whatever, and build their description around that role. The role of the script in a sense is *closed* in that it seems to determine a good deal of the narrative, setting out boundaries and roles and seeming to stand against risk-taking and improvisation. Most importantly, then, the narrative is 'employed' in a scripted manner; it is taken as a major source of guidance, a kind of 'commanding voice' for the living of a life. Description normally implies considerable fidelity to the script that has been embraced, and in most cases the capacity to imagine other lives or situations is thereby somewhat foreclosed. The sense of the life narrative being *closed* is important in not only showing the somewhat determinist nature of a scripted life, but also associated with this is the way in which other possibilities are neither imagined nor subsequently experienced. A scripted description, then, tends to be employed in a closed manner with a minimum of exploration or improvisation.

Description implies, then, a degree of narrative closure. This is what we mean when we say the life stories of scripted describers are in this narrative sense closed. The narrative is not a site of learning, experimentation and open investigation and construction as in other cases. The life narratives of describers recount in a more passive sense what has happened to a person who embraces a particular role or 'birthright'. As a closed kind of narrative it is not a site for the investigation and elucidation of personal agency and action. Rather, it is a place where what has happened is descriptively recounted. Reflecting and internal conversation are seldom evidenced or mentioned in these life story interviews. As a result, narrative intensity is noticeably low and the life story interviews and the life story transcripts indicate a good deal of prompting and probing by the interviewer to elicit information. The life story does not emerge fluently or naturally and consistently stays close to the over-arching script that has been embraced. The absence of improvisation or imagined alternatives gives the descriptions a closed quality. A script has been embraced and other routes or possible lines of inquiry are closed off.

Scripted describers are not at ease with storying their life. It does not come naturally to them. There is little narrative intensity and little evidence that much time has been spent in the course of their life in interior contemplation and narration. This should not be seen as any kind of inferiority, merely a difference from other life storytellers. Scripted describers often have great passion and purpose in their life and their contextual stability adds to some sense of contentment. Whilst John's life is settled occupationally and physically and May, as a traveller, has a nomadic life, both live within a static and well networked community. The great source of stability is the family unit, in particular for John.

Their lives have some sense of agency especially when the inherited script works well, as it does for sustained periods for John. Moreover, instrumental learning takes place throughout the life course. But the absence of narrative elaboration, particularly the fact that self-generated narratives do not develop clear plans of action, means that there is limited flexibility of response to the changing external context. May can see little way out of the 'terrible' aspects of gypsy life. John is similarly a victim when the context is changed. Unpractised in the elaboration of new stories and in developing his own courses of action when the external conditions of farming change, he is unprepared and adrift.

Faced by the new rapacious forces of profit and dispossession, his honourable and 'old-fashioned' morality provides no guidance. Without a history of narrative learning and elaboration, he is powerless in the face of the new social order. When the externally generated script that has been accepted as a life plan is contextually changed, no personal narrative forces can be deployed in the new situation. There is no alternative but to 'keep boogering on'. But in doing this, he is no different to significant swathes of humanity who accept the social script without any personal narrative reaction. Moreover, the difficulties that scripted describers encounter should not be seen as some kind of symbolic dénouement. All patterns of narrativity come with downsides. We must also remember that narrative elaboration does not guarantee wellbeing. I have little doubt that for long periods of his life John, up on the hills on a crisp morning with his cows all around him, was filled with wellbeing – whoever wrote the script.

Scripted describers have less 'narrative intensity' than other groups. They are unaccustomed to talking about, or it seems, thinking about their lives. As a result, their life storytelling is somewhat 'stuttering', with a generally unrehearsed quality. The narrative is less about making sense of a life, rather more about ordering the experiences and factually describing that experience. Scripted describers have a strongly rooted sense of their identity even when in some cases the storytellers are 'travellers'. When, however, change comes it is dealt with inflexibly, for life as it is lived and known has been rooted and routinized, and the capacity to imagine other lives and develop a radically new sense of self has been foreclosed.

The world of May and John that we have briefly examined in this chapter was representative of a major section of the life storytellers who were studied across a range of projects. We could provide hundreds of such examples from the various projects, and we suspect that outside the Anglo-American context this would constitute a dominant type. When the social context is sympathetic to their role, life (and life story) can be sustainable, contented and indicative of wellbeing at its best. However, when the social context is unsympathetic or subject to disruptive change, this equilibrium is rapidly disrupted. This is partly due to the kind of narrativity. Since reflexivity and narrativity are seldom practised, new situations provide challenges for which there is little narrative capital at hand to formulate new views or visions. The high commitment to the birthright, the ascribed role, means that flexibility of response is low.

Early narrative closure means that there is closure of learning potential and of other imagined future courses of action. Where there is learning and imagination, it is focussed primarily on the ascribed 'birthright' role.

In periods of social stability, scripted describers may have sustained self-belief in their identity and work. In periods of rapid social change, the low 'narrative capital' and absence of practice in reflexivity and narrativity mean that minimal flexibility of response is characteristic. A *closed* pattern of narrativity works well in stable social locations, but is ill equipped for a world of fast-paced change and flexibility. Scripted description cannot then be employed to flexibly respond to rapidly changing contexts.

The narrative closure involved in scripted describers' accounts severely circumscribes their 'narrative capital'. Their narrative cannot provide substantial leverage in the delineation of new courses of action that move beyond the original script. Similarly, the learning potential of their narrative capital is linked primarily to instrumental elements of their original script. Finally, the identity potential of their scripted narrative is likewise circumscribed. For instance, only in the last year of his life does John reflect on other ways he could have lived his life. The way the scripted describers' narrative is employed closes off the prospect for broader learning, action and identity exploration and provides low narrative capital for the transitions and critical events of a life.

Chapter 8

Armchair elaborators

Our work on portrayals showed us that not only certain descriptive modes of life storytelling but also some elaborative modes had a *closed* dimension: a dimension that foreclosed the flexible delineation of courses of action.

We have called one group of elaborators 'focussed elaborators' because their capacity to focus is multi-faceted. They can focus on their story with clarity and vision, and this form also allows further benefits, for it leads to clear courses of action and therefore to enhanced agency and efficacy. But elaboration is no guarantee of this multi-faceted focussing.

Many narratives involve the kind of analysis, evaluation and even theorization I have grouped under the title of 'elaboration'. But elaboration itself does not ensure significant focussed action or efficacy. There are a variety of responses to elaboration that lead to other results.

In this regard it is important to distinguish once again between the learning potential of a narrative and its action potential and identity potential (see Goodson *et al.* 2010). Many of the elaborators we worked with employed the full learning potential of narrative activity – that is, they analysed, evaluated and formulated. Their life storytelling was often characterized by fluent narrative flow and by considerable narrative intensity. As a result it seems reasonable to assume that they spent a good deal of time 'in narration', in constructing and fine-tuning their life narrative. In many ways their narrative constituted a 'commanding voice' in their life, but what is stressed is the way the narrative is employed in terms of agency and learning.

The difference between armchair elaborators and focussed elaborators came in the form of their response to these commanding voices. This response differed considerably. Some, for instance John Kentman, whose case follows, were highly narratively intense but sought a life somewhat detached from action. Narration and contemplation, and in his case a 'search for inner peace', became an end in itself. They remind us that a detached link between narration and action itself constitutes a particular vision of agency and human behaviour.

Others were similarly narratively intense but seemed locked into a range of narrative questions that were endlessly revisited. Here, the incomplete formulation of courses of action seemed to be less acceptable than in cases like John Kentman. When talking of activity in the everyday world, the accounts mentioned frustration and a sense of unaccomplished mission. Here, the action potential and identity potential of the life narrative seem to have been incomplete or at least partially unfulfilled. These accounts seem to reflect a desire for greater personal agency and an underdeveloped capacity to forge a link between narrative elaboration and deliverable courses of action. In some cases the courses of action and emplotment can be sketched out and narrated but not actually implemented in the everyday world. For armchair elaborators it would seem that 'finding our story' is one thing but 'living our story' quite another, and the development of new identity projects and new courses of action seem particularly elusive in this group.

John and Paul: armchair elaborators

John Kentman was born in 1948. Because the family home was very small and crowded, when John's younger brother was born, John was sent to sleep at a neighbour's house.

In his 'Auntie's' house, John found welcome solitude away from the hustle and bustle of family life. He spent a lot of time alone, often thinking and developing stories and dreams.

John Kentman was one of the most narratively intense life storytellers. He described himself as a 'searcher'. Early in his 20s, he says: 'I can actually remember searching to find a faith, a belief, a karma if you like.'

He was 'consciously' searching for 'inner peace for, if you like, life … why, I haven't a clue'.

His life has many disappointments and dilemmas – a couple of divorces, the death in a car crash of a much-loved daughter, a range of different jobs in different settings and countries.

Throughout this time his search and narrative elaboration has been a constant feature. In 2000, at the age of 51, he 'was sitting there, one [stammers] one Sunday afternoon, and I suddenly said right out of the blue, I said, "That's it. That's it, I have, I have now had enough, and I shan't go to work." '

So he gave up his job on the railways. He 'went the whole way, and I said "No, you know, let's be me now, let's be the real me." '

He sees himself as a downshifter. Having had some heart troubles, 'I suddenly started thinking, well, should I only have another two years or, or should I go out there now, and there's a big bus comes along, what have I achieved from my own self.'

He adds:

John: I don't see myself solely [stammer] solely as a downshifter. I see it as being perhaps [stammer] a bit of an escapologist, but …
Interviewer: What were you escaping from though, John?
John: I was escaping from the formalities [stammer], the routines [stammer], I felt that [stammer] that I was not a master of my own destiny … Everything I did was for somebody else.

He describes his search as 'the quest to find a better way of life'.

There is a constant search for some sort of peace. In more recent years, John has had a job as a dressing room attendant at a county cricket ground:

[There was] this big buzz going on. And [pause] in the evenings, when all the teams have gone, I'm 99 per cent of the days I'm there, I'm always the last one out the ground, and I sit on the players' balcony, and I have a sandwich, and, and I have a cup of coffee. Er, June time, the sun's just about going down, it's about half past 9 to 10 o'clock, and, er, and it's a lovely evening, and you can see all the trees over the other side of the ground, and I sit there, and I think [pause] 'I've got the kids, I've got a roof over my head [stammer] I've got food in my belly [pause], life is good, you know'. And, er, it's only in the last year, oh dear sorry, I'm getting a bit emotional, it's only in the last year that I've been able to think that [pause]. Maybe in the last two years.

As he says, if 'the reaper' 'came to the door now and said "You've got half an hour, John" [pause], I don't think I'd feel a failure'.

Having been a Christian, although not a believer now, John paraphrases a verse from Ecclesiastes:

'If you wait for, for the wind and the rain and the sun to be exactly right, you will never sow anything and you will never harvest anything,' and so in a way since, since I gave up the railway, I felt to myself, well [pause], you can plan things like, I'll go across and, and I'll see so and so next, next Sunday afternoon, but there are some things where you just think, 'let's see what happens', you know [pause], I'll do it when I think it's about right, you know, not, er, sort of right, let's do it now, but I don't try to over plan any more. And I really like that bit out of Ecclesiastes, er, and I think, although I'm not saying the life I have is, ah, the right life [pause] for the whole world because it absolutely certainly isn't [pause], we all have a buzz out of all various sorts of things, but, but for me I think, I think I did the right things when I did and, and I've been able to get into, a perspective more. It's all, it's like it's been a big jigsaw puzzle [pause] the whole of my life, and it's sort of [pause]. If it was a jigsaw puzzle of a cottage garden, say, er, I think I've done all the nasty bits now, you know [laugh], and it's just, ah, fairly obvious bits.

Giving up work gave John time to be there for his family and to build up family relationships. However, although he likes to spend time at the sports club and with his family:

The nicest days off are often, or, eight times out of every ten, are actually, when I'm [stammer] got a day off at home with absolutely nobody else around. Not even, like, the children of mine, you know.

When asked what is so great about that:

I don't know. [stammer] It's, yeah, I don't know, it's [pause], in some ways it could be that you're not having to put on a show, and that's not saying if I see my daughter or my son that I've got to be the happy daddy, blah, blah, blah, but it is you know [stammer] you can be absolutely natural if you, if you are on your own [stammer] you can 100 per cent be, be how you yourself would want to be, not how somebody else wants you to be.

Towards the end of this interview, aged 55, John says:

I have not given up searching for other things to achieve. I'm not, erm, content with what I've got, and so I've got a list, a list of a few things, but perhaps it's the same with the daily thing, where I've got to sow the seeds, clean the chicken shed, go to bank. You are aware that something else may come up in that time, and so it will either be an extra job that you've got to do or it will be a failure to do all the jobs because you've got a puncture half way down the road, you know. So, if you like, my life is a bit like a meeting agenda, which has got AOB at the bottom, you know, that's that, that's that, that's that, but something else is going to come up. And, a bit like a diary where, if you are a good boss you will, you will perhaps simply diary out five hours a day, leaving three hours for all the things that come up during that day. And, it's a bit like my life. I haven't got a clue as to what it is, but I don't feel content with what I've got yet.

Throughout the interviews, John speaks periodically about himself and his place:

In a way, of the five of us [pause], if a family is a circular table, I'm on the edge of it, er, I'm always on the outside of all the arguments, it all goes on [pause], but I don't come in on them. I'm a fairly, separate person, to all of the rest of them. Um, we're close but I tend to, um, not, not have, a, um, confidentiality with them very often.

   Maybe it's something that has actually gone through the whole of my life, I haven't really felt [stammer] I am where I should be. [stammer] I think that's the right words [stammer] but I'm, [stammer] that I'm actually not [stammer] fully a part of actually what I'm supposed to be in, as marriage, as relationships, blah, blah, blah. [stammer] I've always felt that it's kind of [stammer] of a visiting, er, you know … Yeah, so it has gone through, through the whole of my life that, that kind of a feeling that I'm simply [stammer] passing through something, with the exception perhaps [stammer] of my first marriage where [stammer] where for a fair time I thought that would be the whole of my life.

John reflects back on his childhood, where he created a 'kingdom' he could control, with his train set:

It's quite interesting actually because [stammer] in some ways I'm a bit like that now where I've [stammer] I've formed a style that I like and [stammer] and sometimes I will only allow a person to come a certain amount of the way and then I tend to say that's as far as I want it to go, and the same if I go, if I [stammer] attempt so as to go out of my little circle then I don't seem to feel easy with it. [stammer] Strange. I feel that I've really changed over the years, but if I sit down here and I really talk about it I tend to find that I'm saying [stammer] I haven't changed all that much.

In a sense, you can see John being much in the same solitudinal place begun when living his life on the edge of the family in the house next door. He has never felt: 'I am where I should be.' And though the narrative intensity is considerable, and the narrative search continual, it is the continuities in the courses of action or inaction that seem more salient – the search somehow returns to the starting point. He says this himself – whilst he once searched everywhere, especially for inner peace, he realizes at the end: 'Now I find that it's finding me. And that's nice but it's scary as well.'

Paul Larsen shows many similarities to the case of John Kentman. However, his narrative elaboration is characterized by an extraordinarily high level of narrative intensity and by detailed elaboration and analysis of the most painstaking and continuous kind. Truly, Paul is somebody who lives constantly 'in narration'.

Paul was born shortly after the Second World War into a family of farmers and fishermen in a rural area of Norway. Significantly, the family had strong ties to the Lutheran Free Church, which is a church body characterized by strong discipline and austere visions of lifestyles. From the beginning, Paul sees his story as one where he is misplaced. He calls himself 'a mistake': 'I was born the last of four children, half an hour after my twin brother. They say that I wasn't expected and therefore had no clothes to wear when I came into the world.'

The sense of displacement begins early and it is echoed, not just in his marginal position within the family, but also he feels in his being born in Norway. Again, he regards it is as a 'mistake' that he was born in Norway, 'it was a big mistake'.

This feeling of mistake and location is echoed in his general feeling that in his family situation he was not expected and not wanted. 'So maybe that is an idea that I have used in this conversation that I was born into the wrong place. I shouldn't be but why are people born into places that they shouldn't have been?'

In his early years, Paul regards himself as having been a 'smothered child'. His mother, an anxious and fearful woman, was highly attentive to his every need. His father, on the other hand, was often away and Paul told in his interviews with us of his fear of his red-faced father, of being beaten by him for some of the very minor 'crimes' that he committed as a child.

Paul's escape from this rather unhappy childhood home began when he was befriended by a teacher who taught him to play melodies on the accordion. These melodies focussed on the Sunday school. He says:

> The Sunday school was sort of a real sort of a balm would you say, it was soothing, it was, it was soothing me into, where I could be free of, and that was the other side … Sunday school was that, that as a man I didn't know other than in Sunday school so I could relate to him. He was very, more like a father I would say.

Slowly, Paul began to develop a dream of himself as a teacher, specifically as a music teacher:

> I dreamt to go abroad ... I had a dream, in the college, in the sixth form, to go to Switzerland and study French and music, combine those things, language and music was in my dream ... that was one dream, to go abroad so early I, I, I didn't bind myself to Norway, I'd think of other places in the world.

The pursuit of a career in music as a music teacher provides a strong narrative core to Paul's life story. When he was 19, Paul went to the teacher training college in a distant city on the Norwegian coast.

In due course, he became a college lecturer in music. Paul's girlfriend at the time was training to be a nurse but remained in his home location. Eventually, having been engaged for some years, they got married. This was another act he regarded from early on as a 'mistake', forced on him by his home's expectations: 'It wasn't a marriage, it was an arrangement. It was an arrangement. It was a script ... and in a Christian society you never talked about divorce. That was out of the question.'

However, after 15 years Paul began to rebel against his home location and his affiliation with the Lutheran church. The rebellion was also focussed on freeing himself, at age 35, from the dictates of his father. His father's views and the strict teaching of the church had provided a fairly clearly pronounced and, indeed, patrolled script for Paul's life planning. This script, he now thinks, made him 'much more willing to please other people than finding out what was my needs and my will'.

In this process of becoming and searching, Paul spent a large amount of time 'dreaming' about alternative storylines and narratives for his life. He felt that he should divorce and set off on a new course. For a while, he pursued this new direction, divorcing his wife and leaving behind his four children for a more 'colourful' life in the city where the college was located. He broke away from the church community: 'I started to and, to understand that my life was just, in the Christian world, to do with submission and sticking to the rules.' But still Paul felt misplaced. He still judged that in Norway he 'couldn't be myself'. He grew to believe that you have to 'leave something behind if you ... if you want to start a new chapter in your life'. So Paul began to plan a move to England to study the social history of the music curriculum he had spent so many years teaching. Finally, he succeeded in this goal and came to live in England, to study for a PhD and work part-time as a music teacher. In time, he explored a new partnership and began his new life in England – 'the new chapter' he had dreamt of for so long:

> I guess I, I dreamed a lot, well if you know what I mean, fantasy, dreaming as an inner life, daydreaming more or less. I think I used writing more and more as a daydream. So ... maybe this idea of getting away, getting away from something was, was, erm, came early into my, not consciousness but into my writing, and I think I used music as well as, er, as an escape from, from restraints and, er, rules of

behaviour or whatever we were tied up with, because there were very strict, I would say was rather strict.

His new dream is still locked into resolving the old dilemmas, and constantly in his account he returns to his unresolved relationship with his father and his strict religious upbringing.

In the case of John and Paul, we find highly reflexive and narratively intense life storytellers, but we discern only a tenuous link to the development of courses of action; these are above all armchair elaborators. Their commitment to independence and to a lifelong process of 'becoming' is often very intense, but these seldom translate into a conscientious delineation of courses of action. The process of becoming is therefore closed off, and in this specific sense these narratives are employed as *closed* life narratives. By closing off the active prospect of becoming somebody different, the armchair elaborator forgoes the chance to delineate new courses of action and new identity projects. These alternatives are often speculated upon, even narrated, but never brought into the world of action and self-definition where a new identity is explored that moves beyond the original dilemmas that were experienced.

One of the most complex issues with armchair elaborators is the way their narrative is employed in learning. Often, armchair elaborators are sophisticated and practised in their reflexivity. They know how to elaborately narrate their lives and to reflect upon them. But this reflection has a circular tendency, a way of constantly 'returning to go'. This is because they seem locked into particular passages in their life that they cannot 'go beyond'. As a result, not only do they not imagine new courses of action, their learning is itself sharply inhibited. The problem is most definitely not one of intelligence; in many of our subjects it is more a question of the employment of the narrative in a closed manner. As with scripted describers, there is little open exploration or improvisation in their learning strategies.

Armchair elaboration shows the complexity of 'narrative capital' as the narratives are highly reflexive and sophisticated; these storytellers invest large amounts of time and energy in narration. But the employment of their narratives remains *closed* off from the delineation of new courses of action or the development of new identity projects. Their narrative capital lacks capacity and any strategy for investment in these new initiatives because they remain focussed on earlier traumas or dilemmas. This inhibits their attempts to explore new patterns of selfhood and new modes of learning.

Chapter 9

Multiple describers

The major distinctive feature of multiple describers is that the focus of their life stories involves the choice of, and movement between, roles and identities that are already available within society. But in many ways this kind of narrative focusses on an open exploration of the opportunities on offer. In this chapter we have focussed on two specific categories of exploration to show how these descriptive narratives are used to open up courses of action and learning strategies. We have particularly focussed on two types of *open* exploration: the explorations surrounding the notion of home and ethnic identity, and the exploration of scholarship opportunities, to illustrate the nature of the pattern of learning, agency and identity that are at work.

Identities are embraced as 'off the peg' acquisitions, but the focus of the story is on the ongoing choice of a range of identities. Life story narrations tend to focus on a description of the movement between available identities, whether these be occupational or holistic. In the life story interviews there is low narrative intensity, and little narrative activity is focussed on any personal elaboration or on the personal modification of adopted identities. In general, narrative identities are adopted, not adapted.

This adoption of an off the peg identity could be seen at work in our study of the Greek Diaspora mentioned in Chapter 1. Some people we interviewed who had grown up in America or Germany or Australia with two Greek parents or even with one Greek parent embraced their Greek identity in a profound manner. Fotis talks of his children, parented by him – a Greek man – and his German wife:

> Both my children participate in dance groups and have made many appearances, they know all Greek dances, in other words, they almost do it at a professional level. They keep in touch with Greek music; both my older children play the bouzouki while my daughter has given high level concerts. For instance, once she gave a concert with the Director of the Philharmonic in Berlin. He is widely acclaimed. They presented Theodorakis with an orchestra of about 35, 36 people and my daughter and my son played the bouzouki. My son also plays the violin: my youngest son is learning to play the violin and bouzouki now and he is going to start to dance now as this could not happen before because there wasn't a children's group in the community. They are very active members.

He himself feels his Greekness has intensified whilst living abroad.

> In this way, the Greek element is intensified. I mean, when we go to Greece with these views, we confront a strange treatment. Greeks in Greece don't think in a Greek way, whereas Greeks who live abroad experience this feeling intensely, since they are far away from Greece and live in a different situation: they are interested, they are preoccupied by this, and they find a way. They feel Greek more intensely and they feel that their link with Greece is more powerful. Besides that, there is the issue of racism. While Greeks who live in Greece are obsessed with everything that is foreign, they are more susceptible to racism than the Greeks who live abroad, who may intensify the Greek element, however, they are rid of racist elements. From this point of view, of course it depends on one's intellectual level, I think Greeks who live broad are closer to what ancient Greeks claimed.

Such an embrace of a Greek script is, then, rather 'essentialized', but it represents an imagined yet mobile identity. The power of essentialized notions of identity is considerable and often leads to a well-defined course of action. In scrutinizing people's life stories, it is possible to see how a narrative often represents a 'commanding voice' as to how people act in the world.

During the work on the Professional Knowledge project, I stayed for a period in Gothenburg in southern Sweden. Whilst there, I conducted a series of interviews with Swedes about their conception of Swedishness and home. One of the most interesting interviews was with a young American-born 30-year-old woman – both of whose parents were born in Sweden. The family had settled in Minnesota in America and she had grown up there, but every summer she had been brought to a summer cottage on an island off the coast of southern Sweden. In the family home, whether on holiday or back settled in America, there was an emphasis on bringing her up as Swedish. She was constantly told stories about the Swedish homeland and developed a fairly essentialized notion of herself as Swedish. In this sense, it was very much like the experience of many second-generation Greeks whom we had inter-viewed. What was striking about talking to this young woman, Kirsti, was the relationship between her embracing of a narrative of Swedishness and the course of action that she delineated.

She decided in her late teens that she would return and live on one of the islands off the coast of southern Sweden. So complete was her embrace of the story of the Swedish homeland that she judged this was where she would settle and live out her life. In due course, during one summer she met a local manual worker from one of the islands and she later married him. I spent a day in their delightful home talking about the way in which her embracing of a narrative identity had led to her being settled on this Swedish island. What came over was the way that her imaginary narrative construct of a homeland where she should settle had moved her the enormous distance from Minnesota back to this Swedish island. This search for a homeland is of course a feature of many diasporas – one only has to think of the foundation of the state of Israel or the rumination underpinning the film *Roots* to see how powerful narrative constructions are in the delineation of courses of action.

Another common example of mobile scripts providing an off the peg identity base are people who follow a 'scholarship boy' or 'scholarship girl' trajectory. I mentioned this in Chapter 1, and although I concede an autobiographical predilection for such stories, they do, I think, provide an instructive series of examples.

One of the more common forms of life story and one that characterizes multiple describers is a story of social mobility. Beginning in the 1950s, for instance, there was a commonly used storyline of the scholarship boy or scholarship girl who often achieved great social and often associated geographical mobility. Our study of racial ethno-cultural minority teachers in Canada collected many stories of multiple describers who lived lives of considerable geographical movement and personal development (for a detailed study of a scholarship boy see Goodson in Thiessen *et al.* 1996).

Elizabeth and Charles: multiple describers

Elizabeth grew up in Ghana, a world of scholarship and movement. Having passed an examination to go to secondary school, she had to move away from home.

> When you get to secondary level you probably have to travel about 500 miles away to live in the school. We call it a boarding house, so I lived in the boarding house for the whole five years of my secondary school life.

Significantly, Royston Lambert has called such boarding schools 'total social systems' (Lambert 1968) for they enclose the pupil and provide a total institutional environment and perspective.

Elizabeth, from the beginning then, was defined as a 'scholarship girl' and: 'In high school I did very well, I did very well with my courses, and as soon as I graduated from high school I gained a scholarship to study abroad, that is how I came to Canada'.

The scholarship experience can then be quite easily related in narrative terms – a clear trajectory is provided and in fact a clear accompanying storyline with an established lineage. The storyline provides agency and learning but often forecloses the need for narrative intensity. Hence, in Elizabeth's move to Canada, a great deal of the process of taking up the scholarship was handled by others. Elizabeth saw her task as following the route that was laid out for her: 'We came on a scholarship, we came on a guided plane, then a guided bus and then we were led to this apartment building.'

This did not mean, however, that she saw herself as lacking in personal motivation and agency, quite the opposite. By being able to follow the rules laid out for her she felt empowered. In the move from home to school, from home country to foreign country, she learnt about her capacity to respond flexibly and enthusiastically to a new situation: 'I said I'll handle it, I'll handle anything else. I remember my late uncle saying, "Oh, I know, you'll handle anything," and that was me, I'll handle anything.'

At the centre of her descriptions of her life were her repeated learning experiences. The story tells of her confidence in her personal agency and her capacity to learn in new cultural contexts and new institutional milieux. She says of one such incident: 'All of a sudden you have to learn all of those things ... it was quite exciting ... I got busier and busier.'

Some of our conversations focussed on whether she reflected on her life. I asked, for example, if she had ever kept a journal. She replied that she had very briefly, but that she was always busy learning new skills and undertaking new tasks. Her life was busy and fulfilling and she followed a storyline as a scholarship girl with great fidelity. She is a person of considerable confidence with a sense of purpose and agency. Her descriptions cover a wider range of cultural experiences and myriad new learning experiences.

Like Elizabeth, Charles followed a scholarship route. As we shall see, his case is remarkably similar to the case of George Johnson (Goodson 1996). Johnson followed a scholarship boy route and spent his life pursuing academic success, beginning his PhD in his 50s in an attempt to find a culminating phase to the scholarship route. Besides fidelity to the scholarship story, Charles has fidelity to the notion of homeland identity. This feature of multiple describers was strongly in evidence in our studies of the Greek second-generation migrants referred to earlier. There, migrants followed a spectrum from describers who developed an essentialized vision of Greekness, through to elaborators who had a far more fluid and flexible notion of home and identity.

In Charles' case, fidelity to the scholarship route is allied to a strong commitment to his West Indian identity. The belief in the importance of educational qualifications underpins his life project. After his first degree: 'I did a masters degree, went back to high school where the money was good, and while I taught did another masters degree in education.'

Later on, he wished to go up another step on the educational ladder: 'After teaching high school for a few years, four years or so after that, I thought I needed to go on to the next level and began looking at what I can do to do a doctoral degree.'

Having initially planned to do a PhD in Edinburgh, he later changed plans owing to family reasons, but much later – almost 20 years after his first degree – he enrolled for a PhD at an American graduate school and in due course became an assistant professor of education in Canada.

He is quite clear about finding 'a pathway to a career' as the central motif of his life:

> At the back of my mind I was concerned with social mobility, socio-economic mobility, I was at the base here a young man around 19 or 20 and thought I needed some more mobility and status ... to teach high school then you needed a degree and money, the salary was bigger, you could have done more things, you were a more respected person in the society and that sort of thing ...

Interviewer: Was there a tradition of teaching in your family or was there a tradition of people going to university?

Charles: No, my parents were peasants. Yes, I'm the first generation to go to university because my father was a humble gardener. He had a cutlass or a machete, as they call it here, and my mother did the chores around the house and that sort of thing. I'm from very humble beginnings.

Charles speaks of his being groomed especially by his father to pursue educational qualifications: 'My father was a man who stuck up for me to have an education.' He followed his father's instructions even when he had other dreams as a child. He particularly wanted to be a policeman: 'I liked the uniform and I liked the authority with the law in your hand.' His father said 'no' to this aspiration.

> You didn't talk back, he made a decision and you were going ... Now, if he were a different kind of father who, where I would have had my way, I would never have gone to high school. But he said, 'You are going to high school, my word is the last word' and that's what I did. And when I went, I liked it because I rose and shined at school, you know in high school I got into cliques where the boys, all boys school, we were concerned with excellence, what did you get on the test and how many marks you got there. You got an 'A' here and you got a 'B' there. This is what we talked about ... It was academic work we talked about, we dreamt about, we slept and we, so I ... good group that motivated me as well, because even in the group you were looking for prestige within your group or social group.

The powerful influence of social mobility and status as a life theme and life dream can be seen in these quotes. The associated force of paternal and peer group pressures underpin this embracing of the scholarship life narrative. The scholarship life story is powerfully supported by cultural storylines and by those significant social others: the father and the peer group. This is a script that is socially prescribed, and where Charles' storyline follows the guidelines closely and his father's pronouncements without 'talking back'.

The scholarship trajectory allows Charles to travel the world and become a financially secure professor. But in his ruminations about his West Indian homeland we can see that such multiple and varied narratives come at a price. For he has followed a route where he accepts the identities offered to him as 'birthrights', or as externally generated roles that he adopts and plays, but seldom adapts. His vision of the homeland is similarly essentialized. Talking about his professional life in Canada, he says:

> I guess at a certain extent, part of the problem is me. I'm not a very outdoors kind of person. I have nothing against Canada, just that I guess my past and my upbringing and my tastes have been so ingrained in me that I can't live without touching base with them and, mind you, I have lived in Canada for 18 years ... But the cultural characteristics from H.O.M.E, they've stayed with me and I guess I'm a little more stubborn than some people, you know, to forget some of these things but I can't.

The significant feature of storylines such as those of 'scholarship boys and girls' and essentialized notions of 'home' is that they provide similar narratives across cultures. The literature on scholarship boys in Britain, for example, is immense, from Hoggart's pioneering study conducted in 1957 (Hoggart 1990) through to John Harrison's book *Scholarship Boy* in 1995. Our own research found a wide range of examples of both kinds of storyline underpinning multiple descriptive narratives. George Watson, a life storyteller in the Learning Lives project, subsequently followed a route well beyond a scripted scholarship model, but his early years indicated how powerful early scholarship success could be, particularly for working-class students.

> I was top boy in the, er, in the town, which is why I got my scholarship. There was a top boy and a top girl. That was the 11+ then. Er, I had a very happy time at school. I was far above the rest of my classmates in things like spelling. I read a great deal. So when we had a set book to study I'd usually finished it before we started on it in class, which was a bit boring. Er [pause], no, my family looked on me as a, as a, a genius. Er, I was a spoilt kid I suppose … I didn't have any discipline, at home. I should have had … I was very well looked after at home, and, er [pause], I was never struck by my parents or sent to bed without supper or any of these sort of discipline things. That's what I called being spoiled.

The range of multiple describers covers a wide spectrum of descriptive storylines. We have chosen these particular descriptive stories because such examples can be found across the wide range of cultural milieux investigated. Often, of course, multiple describers embrace other socially constructed storylines. The key point, though, is that their life stories are based on externally generated, socially provided scripts. They may belong to the scholarship scripts that fit a particular moment in history across many cultures, or to specific visions of home and belonging, such as Greekness or the gypsy way of life, or a commitment to particular social or political visions (see Andrews 1991).

In general, though, the storyline draws on a meta-narrative that subsumes the individual in a wider nexus of aspiration and meaning, and one that subordinates elaborated personal visions. Personal visions and dreams can be well conceived and pursued. However, they remain within the frame of the overarching meta-narrative.

Within the parameters of the overarching script, personal agency and the delineation of courses of action can be strongly evidenced; and within the prescribed arenas the person can be well practised in flexibly responding to opportunities, sometimes involving considerable geographical and social occupational mobility. Significantly, though, as we can see in the cases mentioned above, the person holds onto the overarching script as a kind of 'life raft' during the often huge geographical, social and occupational changes and challenges encountered. In this way, personal agency is maximized, but personal elaboration and narrative intensity are much less well developed. The multiple describer can describe a wide range of contexts, changes and challenges, can respond flexibly to new contexts and is practised in new learning. On the other hand, the overriding script tends to constrain personal elaboration and is often defended as a 'life raft' of security with which to face the multiplicity of social and contextual changes and challenges. It is as if the scripts employed may themselves be closed, but the open exploration of their potential and the delineation of flexible courses of action more than counterbalance this pre-closure. The life narratives of multiple describers are stories of open exploration and of a continuous process of aspiration and becoming.

Again, multiple describers illustrate the complexity of the notion of narrative capital. Their capacity to explore openly and to travel the world and move between jobs is considerable. And yet because of the early embracing of a script, whether it be based on ethnic identity or scholarship, there is little cause to imagine or openly explore wider narratives. Multiple describers combine a capacity to flexibly move between job and countries with an incapacity to explore other storylines. Their narrative capital is less substantial when exploring other possible narrative futures. As Charles notes, he once wanted to become a policeman but bowed to the wishes of his father and stayed with the birthright script.

In some of the cases mentioned here, we can see that the early embracing of a narrative has led to a life of open exploration and travel. As long as the central narrative is pursued successfully, the learning, agency and identity potentials are maximized. The price of the fidelity to these narrative scripts is that other narrative futures are not fully explored, and in the case of life storytellers where the narrative is less successful there is less narrative capital available to develop a new identity project or pattern of selfhood. Multiple describers hold onto their central script like a life raft and this is a strategy that – if it works successfully – ensures high geographical and social mobility. The price is a limited exploration of other narrative futures. In this sense, the employment and deployment of narrative is closed, even if played out in multiple settings. The impending danger is that if the central script is suspect to challenge in new economic and social contexts, there is little practice in narrativity or reflexivity to develop alternative courses of action or other identity projects. Without high narrative capital, multiple describers are very dependent on the ongoing viability of their central yet mobile script.

Note

My thanks go to Anastasia Christou for the interview data from the Diasporas project used in this chapter.

Chapter 10

Focussed elaborators

The major feature of focussed elaborators is their concern to break away from inherited scripts or established patterns of socialization. They are characterized by high narrative intensity and spend a good deal of time in reflection or 'in narration'. Whilst most focussed elaborators shared some common features, as we shall see, their narrative responses, and more particularly their elaborated courses of action, varied significantly.

One of the common features of focussed elaborators is an interruption or destabilization of communal or family narratives. This may happen because of geographical movement or social isolation, or at other times because of a critical, sometimes traumatic incident, which ruptures or fragments a deeply held narrative.

These early experiences seem to critically affect the sense of security and contextual stability, and hence the kind of life story that is recounted. As one of our life storytellers said: 'If you can't get it from the outside you have to generate it inside.' When externally produced narratives lose their hold, an internal, focussed drive to develop a new self-generated narrative emerges. This drive to develop a definitive personal narrative can obviously have a range of results covering a spectrum from those I have called focussed elaborators through to the group I call armchair elaborators. At one end of the spectrum, the focussed elaborator develops a self-defined narrative that leads to a course of action, a new pattern of learning and a successfully achieved identity project, sometimes in the form of a vocation – for example, a musician or a puppeteer.

As we have seen in Chapter 8, at the other end of the spectrum the drive for autonomy leads to a series of narrative constructions, none of which leads to a systematic course of action, pattern of learning or new achieved identity. Sometimes the life storyteller argues that this is the point – to just 'live' and not be endlessly striving – but the intensity of their narrativity and their drive for personal meaning seem to be at odds with this existential story.

Let me now deal with the group of focussed elaborators who define a narrative that is closely linked to a life project or detailed course of action. Because of this central link, we have at times called this group 'primal' or 'autonomous' elaborators because of their central agentic drive for a newly constructed life project. Whilst recognizing that autonomy in the fullest sense is impossible, and acknowledging that much of their storying involves employing parts of existing storylines and scripts, nonetheless autonomy in the sense of 'functioning independently' or 'self-governing' is a clear common goal in this group.

In terms of narrative intensity, the would-be autonomous focussed elaborators are very clearly practised and adept in narration. Their narratives provide a wide socio-cultural setting for their stories. Their stories are located historically and sociologically, and there is often an underpinning theory to how the story is constructed and told.

Csíkszentmihályi and Beattie have described this push for a theory of living as a life theme:

> A life theme is defined as the affective and cognitive representation of a problem or set of problems, perceived or experienced either consciously or uncon-sciously, which constituted a fundamental source of psychic stress for a person during childhood, for which that person wished resolution above all else, and which thereby triggered adaptive efforts, resulting in attempted identification of the perceived problem, which in turn formed the basis for a fundamental interpretation of reality and ways of dealing with that reality.
>
> (Csíkszentmihályi and Beattie 1979: 48)

Aware that this can come across as rather jargon-ridden psychologese, they helpfully add:

> In a more compressed form, the definition would read: 'A life theme consists of a problem or set of problems which a person wishes to solve above everything else and the means the person finds to achieve solution.'
>
> (ibid.)

The pattern of development of life themes was originally suggested in their longitudinal study of artists. Creative artists, they found, 'use the medium of visual representation to help themselves discover, formulate and resolve in symbolic form some central existential concerns which were causing intra-psychic stress' (ibid.). The artists themselves often expressed this in slightly more vernacular form. Take Tracey Emin, one of our most gifted creative artists. She recently wrote about the juxtaposition of life themes and art:

> Apparently I'm a pendulum: fat to thin. When I'm unhappy, I'm too thin, and when I'm unhappy, I'm fat. There have been only the briefest moments in my life when I have been at the correct weight, even as a child. So I have had to sit down and track the good-looking moments and see if they correlate with being happy. Of course, they do, as the fat and the thin fall nicely into place with the depression and sadness. Apparently that's why I drink, to fend off all the emotions. Then, like some fucking great volcano I erupt when it's least expected, spilling my shit and pus and hell onto anything and everyone close to me.
>
> All obvious, but sometimes in life we need to be told – and most importantly, we need to hear.

I so much want to see and experience the world as a beautiful place. I'm tired of the hurt – even walking and thinking hurts me – but I know I'm very lucky. I'm an artist. That means I can bundle all this stuff up, put it on to a trolley, wheel it out of my sodden mind and straight into the gallery of the world. I can turn it all into a real thing. A thing of substance, a thing called art.

(Emin 2007: 6)

Christopher: focussed elaborator

Focussed elaborators are practised in the narration of their lives. Talking to Christopher is like joining an ongoing and intense conversation. He seems closely in touch with his feelings and thoughts at each moment of the interview. He is sensitive to feedback but has a clear path and plot for his story and will not brook too much redirection or intervention. There is a well worked out 'spine' to his story, and it is so closely interlinked with his sense of identity and agency that the whole story forms an indistinguishable whole, comprising his story, his selfhood, his identity and his actions. The story may then seem self-centred but is in fact anything but, for he draws on examples from literature, philosophy, art, social science and psychotherapy as well as on the experiences of others. His story is an elegant combination, then, of 'internal affairs' and 'external relations'.

As will be seen later, Christopher's life story – or at least his identity – has a central theme: the gay puppeteer (though early in the first interview he is keen to critique the notion of such generalized labelling as limiting/constraining). As a puppeteer, his life's work has involved storytelling. He reflects:

I think reality is dawning on me now that a lot of what I've done in my life has been around fantasy, has been around creating, creating, erm, what's that thing, what's a chimera, is that something that is like, you think it'll be there but it won't be there, is that what a chimera is?

Interviewer: It is, yeah. A sort of symbolic universe.
Christopher: I think that's kind of what I've been chasing and creating. And all these things, which I think are valid, I do feel that, when I look at them I still feel, yes, that's good. But, erm, I'm wondering if, as you say, all the reason for reinventing myself is, is different now. I'm not sure whether it's the same.
Interviewer: Why is it different now? I resonate with what you're saying, but why is it different at this age and stage to before when reinventing allowed you, in a sense, to go on with your trajectory, what's different now?
Christopher: Yeah, I'm wondering if reinventing kept me away from some aspect of reality. You know, the fact that I immerse myself so deeply in fantasy, and creating art through that ... I feel that if there is a falling away of some of this fantasy, this need to create another

world, and I feel that when, if part of this is probably kooky, a kooky idea, that if I can let some of it fall away, what will fall away, what will be left and what will fall away will still have a validity, you know, it's like, erm, I don't feel that, I feel that I can learn from the work that I've done somewhere, I feel I can plough it back in, in some way and maybe there's a learning I could make from the work that I've done … what I'm saying is that I think that the process of my career as an artist has been [pause] … a process of, of deepening my life, and therefore that's not invalid. You know, OK, so I have created a fantasy world in many ways, but in the sense that a myth has, has a real sort of truthful side, a learning, you know, it's possible to learn through myth, I think that the story of my life through the work that I've done, there's something for me to learn from it, I feel that somewhere.

For Christopher, the 'narrative', the 'myth' is absolutely central to his life.

I have a strong sense of the mythic and the fairytale and the, not magic, but the powers beyond just the everyday, which is part of, you know, I feel as if the whole dream/reality thing is part of, deeply part of me.

From the age of two and a half years old, he feels he has 'had to invent myself'.

And he goes on reinventing. After interview nine, he phones the next day to say that he has been thinking about the interview. The message he leaves is that the moments of life when he feels he has fallen into a pit are about life saying to him that he must 'reinvent', 'rediscover', 'resee' himself. These, he goes on to say, are 'moments in life where he has had to make those growth steps'.

This persistent invention is what I call *re-selfing*. In the new age of life politics we are increasingly challenged to keep changing (Obama's mantra is 'time for change'). But the new economy demands that people change and re-skill many times over in their work life course. Hence, the re-selfing accompanies the new age and the new economy. In Christopher's case, as he enters a new transition he talks of 'a new Christopher' being constructed and then emerging. This re-selfing is surely a perceptive strategy – many longevity studies of people who live long and creative lives talk of people living 'a succession of lives'. In other words, these people – like Christopher – become practised in re-selfing.

The ease with which Christopher recounts his story implies a good deal of interior thought and reflexive rehearsal.

He was born during the Second World War into a middle class family in Southern England. There was, he believes, a 'golden time' for the first months of his life.

There's a picture of my mother holding me as a very young child, when I was quite newly born, and there's a photograph she'd written on the back to send to someone, this is, this is my new child Christopher, something like isn't he sweet,

or isn't he lovely or something, written on the back. So I think at some, when I
was very young I was loved, very much, by my mother.

There was, in the photograph, 'real warmth, and the way she'd written this on the
back. It was obviously genuine you know'.

Fifteen months after the birth of Christopher, his mother gave birth to another
son, changing the family dynamic and providing competition for Christopher. By
the time Christopher was two and a half years old, his parents parted and divorced.
Up to that point, although he thinks he may be able to remember 'terrible rows'
between his parents, his 'myth' is that this was a period of 'safety':

> That's the feeling. It was safe up to there ... I feel I was loved, and I feel as
> though I know, I know what it feels like to have been loved, and I think if
> I hadn't known that, I could be a drug addict, I could be a delinquent, I could be
> a criminal, I don't know what I could be, but because of that, that redeems me.
> That's my feeling.

His mother remarried; Christopher and his stepfather were unable to build a close
father–son relationship. His mother ultimately sank into alcoholism and agoraphobia.

> I can remember the daily grind of living in a place where, which was out of joint,
> and where love was not a generous commodity, it wasn't there on tap. And
> Mother had to hide in a way, had to be sort of, just through there, in order to be
> loving, not be in the room with you.

He was sent to a private prep school. Interestingly, Christopher does not tell of his
time at this or subsequent schools (other than that it was reported that he was a 'trial
and a tribulation'). The school was based on the philosophy of Charlotte Mason.
Two aspects of her philosophy may be of special note in this narration. First, she
believed that it was important to tap into the 'talking resource' of children, con-
sidering their talk to be the art of narration. She had the notion that narration invited
a child's personality to become part of her/his learning process. Second, she believed
that in a structured, supported way, it was best to leave children to learn 'naturally',
sometimes with little or no intervention from adults. There was also a strong
parent–school association. Additionally, and appropriately for Christopher's life
story, the school had the motto: 'I am, I can, I ought, I will.'

From about the age of eight, when he discovered puppets, Christopher, it seems,
began a lifelong occupation (vocation) in puppetry.

At primary school, when Christopher was seven or eight years old, a fellow pupil:

> had a little articulated doll ... I really wanted it ... it was a little jointed figure and
> I loved that little jointed figure that this person had ... I think the fact that it had
> little joints, I loved the fact that you could move it. So it wasn't just like a teddy
> bear, it was also something you could move and you could change its aspect, and

I think that there was already probably the beginnings of wanting to imprint myself on the outer world through using objects ... it feels like I was taking a seed in from those early adorable objects, that I was taking something inside myself, planting a seed, I mean that little figure, that little Hrvnek figure, which was this adorable, he had clogs on and was a little Czechoslovakia, and, and I think Pinocchio, Pinocchio has that, the little jointed legs and everything, and I think I adored that. And I think it was like something, almost taking the seed in to me.

By the age of nine or ten he 'was clearly passionate about puppets'. He learned that he could, through his puppets, 'articulate living, of course a puppet isn't living, I know that, but I could bring it to life. I learnt that quite soon by my little toy Muffin the Mule. So, I was, I knew that there was this love, love affair with these puppets.' Puppetry, at this early age, he remembers:

gives me all my quirkiness and my mythicness and it seems to satisfy a lot of the needs that I seemed to have as a human being at that time. I think the fact that puppetry are quirky and strange and jerky and cheeky and all the things, in a way I've put a lot of my stuff into that ... So I discover something very important at that stage, which is going to put me on a trajectory.

But it is a trajectory to somewhere, rather than a definitive goal to be attained. There is ambivalence:

When I was probably 12 or something, I used to, in the ... library they had a section just right at the bottom for puppets, some things on puppets, and it was right at the bottom of the shelves so you could sit on the floor and enjoy the books, it was great because you could be just very intimate with these little books which I loved ... one of them was of this puppeteer ... it had lots of photographs of his puppets and I remember thinking, just loving these puppets, the beauty of them, the craft of, the craft of them, and thinking wouldn't it be wonderful if I could make puppets like that one day?

From about the age of nine, Christopher began to be involved in activities which supported puppetry. There is a:

list of things which I did in my teens, all to do with theatre and around the stuff that I do now ... I think it's remarkable, when I look at this list which I've brought along, of the things, how, you know, out of nothing, I, what I did with no tutor or anything, you know, I didn't have any tutor at all ... at the age of 11,12, 13 and I was putting together a whole career, a whole way of life.

I know at that point, from that point on, right the way through my teens and really right the way through my life ... I set myself on a trajectory which I really worked at ... there's a huge list of things which I ... projects that I did. And it feels like I was *really* working hard towards it, so it feels like that at the, really working hard to, to put something, to create something, of, of my situation.

So much of the narrative activity Christopher recalls is internally driven – there is continual evidence of an intense preoccupied interior conversation. Hence, there was no clear path for Christopher in his relationships with others: 'in interaction with people, I just had *no* language, no way of, of being with people, I was shy, I was anxious, er, erm, and I was, erm, I sort of cut myself off'.

At school, Christopher was exploring relationships with boys and girls. At art college:

I had a girlfriend there … and we had some pretty great adventures. Exploring being straight or being gay. I mean, I knew at school that I loved, I don't know if I should be saying this, but I loved the sexual encounters with the boys there. I'm sure a lot of kids do. Anyway, I did. But then I was, I was exploring being straight, you know, I had this girl … friend, and we had all kinds of adventures and it was sexual too … I think I was sort of learning about one-to-one relationships.

Following the death of his mother, Christopher found himself in 'a terrible mess'. Already in a relationship, he met and fell in love with a gay Irish Catholic man. He let the relationship run its course and, perhaps for the only time in his life, might have been prepared to abandon his work for the sake of the love affair. Ultimately, Christopher found himself living alone and chose to take a course of action which was to result in him moving on from the shy, anxious phase of his life, but this plan of action only occurred when Christopher was in his 30s. It involved intensive therapy, and although he no longer attends regular therapy he does elect to take part in therapeutic workshops and has found a co-counsellor recently to help him work through his story.

During the course of the Learning Lives project, Christopher's long-term partner left him for another man.

So part of what I want to do now is to, not exactly reinvent myself, but rediscover myself as a, as it were, in quotes, 'single man'. You know, maybe I'll have a partner again in a little while, but maybe I'll, you know, I want to know what it is now to do, to do this … it feels like I have a, quite a, a lot of abilities, so it feels like, erm, I, maybe it's having the courage to wait and discover where, where it is to go now.

Not only did his partner leave him but there was a disagreement with a long-standing friend that resulted in the breakdown of the friendship, and another friend of many years became ill and died. Christopher found himself once more alone, as in childhood.

Christopher: So here I am in a temporary accommodation with someone who's very nice to me, very, er, supportive, but not a friend in the sense I've only met him through this accommodation, and I'm about to buy a new flat and it feels like it's a big, restarting of my life in a way. In a new way, without a partner and without two very important people in my life. And I'm, sometimes I think what is that telling me, what is life inviting me to do next? That's a learning.

Interviewer: And have you come up with any kind of answer to that?

Christopher: My feeling at the moment, it's quite strong and clear, is that it's almost like I just need to contain all these things in myself and wait. I do feel that. It's almost like it has to be, like in a, like in a pot or a bowl inside me. It's not cooking, it's just sitting, and, erm, I, it would be wrong to pre-empt it in any way. I feel there's a lot of stuff there that, if I'm patient and can have the strength to just contain it, hold it, could be very rich. But it's not easy because it's lonely, being without these people and without what was my home, you know. So it feels [pause], it feels emotional, really.

Temporarily this lonely state 'feels a bit like the project I'm on at the moment, erm, it's like, exploring life alone'.

My whole life is changed … it just feels like I'm, I'm literally finding a new Christopher. Not a new, a new Christopher, er, no, not a new Christopher because, erm, obviously, I think the Christopher is the same, but it's like a new way, a new, it feels like a new chapter of my life has opened up and I'm, I'm starting this new chapter, and it's, the pages in the future have no writing on them. Whereas I think up to the point at which I separated, the pages on the next few pages did have writing on them, because I had a projection of where I would be going, what life would be like. But now I don't … it feels like I've become quite porous to life now, and I feel like I'm, I'm soaking in life again, and it feels like, erm, in order to, to, to give myself a maximum opportunity to, to move into the next place. That's what it feels like … I feel that I'm open at the moment, and that feels like, er, there are places where I can look at again which I haven't perhaps looked at … I'm much more open to, to things emerging out of whatever is, whatever is there in front of me or around me.

Part of him wants to find a new partner and enter a new relationship, but he feels that by stopping being alone he 'would be escaping something very important'. So he is:

facing up to the fact that I feel ultimately completely alone. Absolutely alone, and, and this has some, and I think of death … I do think that that is, the one thing that we experience utterly alone is the experience of death, and I feel that, so maybe I am experiencing some kind of experience of death at the moment. It's the death of a relationship. And I think in some ways it feels like the death of a life, in a way, I feel that [pause] I was thinking just this morning I think, as I was getting up, I was thinking how many unfinished projects I have in my life, masses of unfinished projects, and I thought, well, maybe my life is an unfinished project. Maybe at the end of my life it will be an unfinished project.

By the next interview, things have changed again and now he is in a new relationship and feeling fit and healthy and full of vigour.

Christopher's story ultimately seems like a quest for spiritual wholeness, wisdom and integrity: 'all my life I've, I've been intrigued and fascinated and tempted by the, by the solitary life, by the life of a monk or a hermit. I always found that very beautiful'.

When Christopher was established as a puppeteer there was a period of work on saints:

> The thing of doing stories of saints is something which, I think is looking, it's, it's actually looking for the saint within oneself ... looking for that purity, that, erm, quality of the miraculous that I think we all have and that I think I see in puppets, the simplicity of the puppets has that saintly quality, it has also the opposite, it has the ... diabolic as well. And that's the shadow side, which is, and I have that too.

By his early 30s Christopher:

> was trying at the time to practise spiritual, you know, I was trying to meditate, I was doing tai chi, I was reading a lot, trying to do a lot of kind of, I began going to church as well, I was trying to do some kind of spiritual practice, but I was very spasmodic, I'd do a bit of this, then I'd not do it, then I'd, oh, I'm meant to be doing that, you know, and one day I thought, well, why not, why not do the, put the ...? One thing I do at, on a regular basis is work on my, my art. I don't have any difficulty in doing that, I don't lapse with that ... why not put the two together, so say the spiritual is in harmony with the work, it's, after all life is only a certain length and maybe there isn't time to do all these other things and maybe one has to sort of dovetail, that was what I was thinking.

Now in his mid 60s, Christopher reflects on life plans, trajectories, quests and goals. He believes that everybody has a 'trajectory' for his or her life:

> I don't think trajectory is something you decide, I think it's something that, that happens to you from almost the moment of birth. Has to do with karma and all these things, it has to do with that, that it's not, I don't actually believe in predestination or, or that, but I, I think there is something *in* the power of the trajectory and I do think that, I don't believe that people don't have trajectories.
>
> They say that, that every family, every child is put on a trajectory of life, you know, I think it's a bit like the family pull the bow back with the child and aim the arrow in a certain trajectory and then let it go, with the child, and then the rest of the life of the child has to do with that trajectory, that the parents have sort of established. I think there's a lot of truth in that.

But Christopher also feels a need to *do* something about difficult situations:

> I don't think I've ever felt that I was born to be, erm, a criminal or a, I don't think I have, although I have, you know, when I walk past someone sitting on the street,

you know, with a begging bowl, I do genuinely feel there but for the grace of God, I really do, I feel you're only that far away from me, I'm only that far away from you, I know where you are, but I also now know, it's like Christ's thing, you know, erm, whatever it is, heal thyself, no, what is it, pick up thy bed and walk, and I know what that, I know what the difference between collapsing on the street and asking for money, and getting up and walking on in life is. And I sometimes feel, when I see these people, just like saying, just get up and walk, *go*.

I think I've always wanted to make the very, to say make the best of my life, it doesn't quite feel like that because I don't feel like it's a, it's a, a plan I could draw up, it's like, it feels like what I want to do is, is, it's a bit like when you go into the sea, and you push and you feel, against the water walking out, and you feel you're pushing in through, through the water out to sea as you walk into the deeper water. That's what I feel a little bit, life with me, it's like I'm wading into life, so I couldn't really say exactly where it, where it, or what it is but it feels like what I've, what I've always wanted to do is, is take the next step into that, that ocean or whatever it is, it feels a bit like that.

I mean, my journey seems to be towards some kind of fulfilment, some kind of completeness, some kind of togetherness with myself and with the world.

Christopher's story is one of unification, 'wholeness' and transcending worldly living. He uses his puppets as:

some kind of cement, not a cement, some kind of linking factor, that they can take on any role, I can make, I feel now that the puppets [beep] but the puppets, it's almost like they can, I feel now overtly that the puppets are part of me, you know, that they are fragments of my psyche … I've never, ever wavered from puppets, I've never wanted to do, I've never, ever been, had the feeling, I want to do something else, *ever*, ever, ever. And I know people who have started on something, say, 'Oh, we gave that up.' Sometimes I've thought, recently I've thought, well maybe there will come a time when I will no longer do the puppets. I will do something else, I will be beyond the puppets or something …. But you see, if I've dropped out, and I have occasionally, I've thought, well, I'll do something, I'll do music or I'll do whatever, I've ploughed it back in, so once I've dropped out, I then put it back in the puppet thing and turn it over again, it's like riches, enriches the soup, the puppetry soup.

Asked if he has ever doubted his return to puppetry when he has taken time out, he responds:

Never, never, never. Never, never, never. But just recently I've thought, well, there may be a time when the puppets, I no longer do the puppets any more. I've always thought I'd always have a workshop 'til the day I die. And just occasionally I've thought, well, maybe I won't need one until the day I die. I don't know what that means. Maybe I'll find some way of transcending the puppets. But at the moment, I feel that there's so much juice, so much richness in my relationship with them and, and what we offer each other, what they offer me and what I offer them in terms of my, it has been my career, but also in terms of my personal development.

He feels that he has brought together his artistic and spiritual journeys, although he has been less successful in integrating his relational with his occupational/spiritual journey. In his current relationship, he feels that this may be about to change.

Indeed, in the very last interview Christopher's view begins to change very markedly. He begins finally to assess his life project – and the parts of himself that it has excluded and imprisoned. The great virtue of a sustained collaborator is that aspects of the life course and life cycle can be seen in operation during the course of the four-year research project. He notes that he is ending 'in a different place from when we started':

> Yeah, it has, it's come at a time, a hugely changing time for me and also it's a time when I think changes are happening to me that I had no idea would happen. I think I'm in, really in a different place now than I was when we started. And I think these interviews have been part of that whole process, they have sort of, is it informed that process, or is it just, erm, somehow the fold-back, reading the stuff has been very good for me in this time.

Interviewer: I've got two questions here, I mean, one, you say it's a period of huge change. How does it compare with other periods of huge change that you've been through, because you've been through a number of transitions, haven't you?

Christopher: I have. I think that one of the big things is that the whole art thing is now being questioned for the first time in my life. You know, the idea of my being an artist, what it is to be an artist, and it comes back to a lot of the things in our interviews, where I've talked about the reason for being an artist, and your marvellous thing of the [pause] oh, what's it called, the thing into gold, lead into gold … Alchemy?

Interviewer: Alchemy, yeah.

Christopher: Alchemy. And I do think that's what happened to me. And I think, I think, erm, I think I've used my whole art throughout my life, I've used it as an escape hatch, as a place to go when things got really hard. And I think in there has been, although I *do* think I have a *really*, a real vocation, I really think I have something to offer as an artist, I really do think I'm a true artist, I also think that through that I have actually missed out on a tremendous lot, or somehow sidestepped commitment to a lot of things that aren't to do with art.

Interviewer: Take us through it.

Christopher: Mainly to do with relationships.

Interviewer: Can you take us through that, though, what the sort of …?

Christopher: Relationships mostly.

Interviewer: Do you think so?

Christopher: Yeah. I know I've said it previously.

Interviewer: You have said it before.

Christopher: I've said that I've always, you know, if I'm in a relationship with you, then I always know, just here in my mind [chuckles], that my workshop's there, so if you let me down, if you do a runner, if you do what my dad did, I can go there. And I've had that always, to work, to the work, I've had that, I've used it all the time, and I think now this is the first time in my life where I don't seem to be doing that. It seems to be different.

Interviewer: Why do you think that is?

Christopher: I think it's something to do with the last, when we first met up, I had just broken or was in the midst of breaking with my big relationship.

Interviewer: I think that was the second interview, yeah.

Christopher: Yeah. And at the time I was, I think I was just clobbered, I was just, erm, whatever it is, you know, what is it when you're hit, and I didn't know what was happening. But I realize now that it's a huge change that has been, it feels like it. Who can say, it may not be, but it feels like it is, and it feels like a lot of all that needs to be assessed, the whole thing of what I've been doing with my life. There's a little bit of grieving because I'm 65 now and am thinking, well, and I'm thinking also there's a lot of work, I've got trunks of puppets that are unfinished projects that I've gone into *whole*-heartedly, you know, I've probably told you that there was one play I did, I did almost the complete range of puppets which were about four feet high and I then decided they were all too big, so I started to carve the *whole* lot at about half their size, you know, and all these are in trunks because I never finished the project in the first place, in the end anyway.

Interviewer: And what are you saying that makes you feel?

Christopher: What I think I'm saying is that, that I think [pause] that me being, my art, my being an artist is part of, was part of my stumbling in life, or *is* part of my stumbling in life, and, erm, so it's not surprising there are unfinished projects, things that I've sort of gone into, is it this place, do I, is this the place, it's almost like *is this* the place where it will *really* happen?

Interviewer: What was it you thought was going to really happen? What was it that you were looking for, going down those routes?

Christopher: I think at one level I wanted to be a great international artist, and I sidestepped that and I don't think that, that lessens me as an artist, because I think I am the true, the real McCoy, but I think that part of me would have liked the swagger of being 'I am' in the puppet sphere, 'I am', yeah, I'm pretty, people know, people, 'Oh, Christopher, oh, right', and that definitely is the case, you know, and that's nice. But I think part of me would have loved that. But that would also have been in a way saying to all my past, my family, you know, *look*, I don't need you, *this* is what I can do, you know, I can do *this*, and look how good I am, look, everybody's talking about me, you didn't. So there's a bit of that, a bit of ...

Interviewer: So is it partly a quest for autonomy, then, I mean, this is a word we've used in some of our things, that when you say it's an escape hatch, if the person lets you down, you can go there, is it, I mean, we're trying to get at what that search is.

Christopher: There's a lot of sadness in the studio, and I'm beginning to see that. The, the, I'm lonely when I'm working, because it's a solitary life, I'm on my own. And I love being with people, I love being with people who I love and who love me. So, your question was?

Interviewer: Is it about autonomy?

Christopher: Autonomy?

Interviewer: You know, in a sense separating yourself from others? Was that the original search and are you questioning the original search, I suppose I'm asking.

Christopher: I think it's not exactly autonomy, because I think this thing of the escape hatch, I have felt and I still feel a sort of, a burning sense of love in that art process, and so I sort of feel it is a substitute love, in some way. And I suppose also the puppets can't reject me, so if you reject me, I'll go somewhere where there is love generated.

Interviewer: But you're controlling it.

Christopher: But I'm, I'm controlling it, yeah, I am controlling it, but I do feel there's this resonance because, as I've talked in other interviews, I think that the actual art work, yes, it is being controlled by the artist, but in some ways it's not being controlled, because it is, it's happening along a line of exploration that doesn't have a pre-planned route, so it's not, it's not, erm, do you know what I mean? It's like ...

Interviewer: I do, yeah.

Christopher: There's an element of, there's a huge element of, oh, wow, there, we're there now, you know, and different, that's quite different. So there is that. So it isn't just about autonomy. And I'm feeling more and more that autonomy isn't really the thing, I'm questioning the whole thing of, I've done years and years in therapy. I'm not questioning the fact that it was very valuable at the time, but it feels like the spaces I seem to be wanting to go to now, the therapy thing which is about, seems to be about functioning, for me and in society, you know, getting my life together so that I can function, seems to be less and less, somehow, important, it feels like there's something, there's a deeper place to go now. And I think in this new relationship with Chris that I've talked about a number of times, I think this is almost, possibly because of our talks, and maybe this whole journey that I've been doing, it feels like here I'm *not* using it, art, as an escape route, I'm practically not creating at the moment.

Interviewer: Is that a source of sadness itself, not to create?

Christopher: No, it isn't. I mean, yes, it is a difficult thing because I am conditioned and hard-wired, as they say, to, to create, to, to work, you know, I'm, I'm a worker, not exactly '-aholic', but I'm a worker, generator fellow, and so I think there is, there is a feeling of, I should be working, I should be producing something, there's nothing to show for today, you know, if I haven't, if I've nothing to show for today, then maybe today doesn't exist, you know, I haven't really paid my way or I haven't, you know, validated myself in that day.

Interviewer: Has there ever been a period before where happiness in the relationship has allowed you to suspend that hard-wiring?

Christopher: Erm, yeah, I wonder [pause], I've been thinking back and reading the transcripts and seeing that, I can't really, don't really know if there was, I wonder if there was any in the childhood [pause], you see, I'm seeing now that I'm actually, I think I've denied my sexuality a tremendous, not my gendered sexuality or whatever, but the fact that I'm a very sexual man, and I've just denied that a lot and I've put it in a very much a, that's sex and this is spirituality, this is art, this is love, and I've kept the two apart. Feels like I'm not doing that at the moment.

Interviewer: So talk about the sadness in the studio now, then.

Christopher: It's loneliness.

Interviewer: Never confronted it before?

Christopher: I confront it every time I go in the studio.

Interviewer: Have you always thought it's lonely?

Christopher: I think I have, but because of the feeling of, of the sweetness of the product, the stuff that has been generated, which is genuinely good, you know, I know that, and therefore, and I've felt that as I've done it, so I suppose that's compensated, but, yes, I think I, perhaps I've denied the loneliness. I think I've denied it.

Interviewer: Why can you confront it now, then, I mean, that's what's interesting, isn't it?

Christopher: [Sighs] [pause] Yeah I don't know why I can confront, why do I confront it now? It feels like I've, maybe, maybe it feels like that up to now I've *tried every* which way to make it all work, you know, relationships, my work as an artist, my career, all the stuff I do in my life, and it just somehow hasn't worked. The thing with the split up with Robbie was a *big* thing, because I really felt that that was. And now, looking back on it, I think, what a crazy idea to think that this was for all time, you know. You know, there were so many, it feels so right now that we're separated. And though there were so many things in the relationship which we hadn't, we weren't sorting out and we weren't talking about. Yes, we still love each other very deeply, but at the time we were, we weren't sorting things out and, erm, I keep going off the point and then losing the track of the question.

Interviewer: The only question was, you know, you say you're confronting the loneliness of the studio, the loneliness, in a sense the loneliness of creativity, but my question was, had you not confronted that before?

Christopher: I haven't.

Interviewer: No.

Christopher: I think I haven't. Somewhere, is the word sublimated, it in the work, somehow the satisfaction of the work, and the feeling that when I come out of the studio I should take stuff out and people will love me for my work. It's almost like, if you don't love me now, I'll go there and I'll create something and then when I bring it out they will love me. And so there is a feeling of a tremendous, er, output or outpouring of love in the studio, and I think it's partly in order to get the love back when people say, 'Oh, look at this, how clever'. And that was, that's kids' stuff, I know that comes from my youth, you know.

Christopher, through his creativity and creative self-building, goes on developing his understanding of himself and his social context. He is still vigorously involved in 'the process of becoming'. As with other focussed elaborators, and similarly to Eva Freud who was featured in Chapter 5, he develops an open narrative that will allow him to pursue the process of becoming: 'my journey seems to be towards some kind of fulfilment, some kind of completeness, some kind of togetherness with myself and the world'. Christopher employs and deploys his narrative to develop an open delineation of courses of action and learning strategies. He talks at various stages of there being a 'new self' emerging, 'a new Christopher'. He is prepared to follow this to conclusions that question and in the end reposition his work and his relationships. As with multiple describers, the central script has been a life raft, however, Christopher has employed it to pursue a lifelong journey towards completeness and transformation. In the later stages of his life, he is patently more concerned with relationships and sociability, and this is a long-distance journey from his family beginnings. He conceptualizes these transformations as the birth of a 'new self', and observing him over the four years of the project this could be clearly evidenced. In the next chapter, we examine this concept of re-selfing and its implications for the direction of our economic and social future.

In the final chapters, we are concerned to examine what our studies of narrative character might indicate about capacities to negotiate the rapidly changing contemporary world of flexible economies and technologies. Which narrative characteristics might be most suited for the world of consumption, twitter and blogosphere, the world of short contracts and serial short careers, the world of short-termism, immediacy and economic migration?

This seems to be a world where re-selfing will be an urgent and continuous requirement, and where narrative capital will have to be deployed and employed in the task. Focussed elaborators do seem well equipped for these likely social and economic futures. Their capacity to define life themes that delineate courses of action and new identity projects and relations can be clearly evidenced. Their high narrative capital means they are practised in the reflexive definition of new narratives and in the utilizing of these narrative resources to respond to transitions and critical events. The fact that Christopher conceptualizes a new self for a new transition – a 'new Christopher' – indicates an acute awareness of this process. He is willing to question the assumptions and vocation underpinning his earlier narrative as he confronts the transition to older age. As we have noted earlier, retirement and old age provide a sea-change in most people's lives, and we can see how the practised elaborators employ their narrative capital to envisage new courses of action and new identity projects. In the next chapters, we speculate further on the implications of types of narrativity for the new social and economic future.

Chapter 11

Reflexivity, re-selfing and hybridity

In the previous chapters we have seen how different narrative styles craft varied patterns to portray selfhood and identity. We must, however, be wary of overestimating the continuity and stability of narrative characterizations and patterns of selfhood. Quite clearly, 'the self is or can be many different things at any given point in time or period in a person's life' (McAdams 2001: 116). As a result, our narrative characterizations of selfhood are themselves subject to change and discontinuity.

One of the ongoing debates in social analysis is about the degree of this change and discontinuity. Post-modern theorists incline to a view that each identity project is underpinned by a shifting and multiple set of narratives. Some argue against the existence of an impulse for coherence and continuity. They judge that narratives seldom provide integrative accounts which form coherent bases for selfhood and identity.

This view can be evidenced in some of the research reported, and most certainly life storytellers sometimes shift between elaboration and scripted description. We are not describing pure or absolute types. Sometimes, we seem heavily involved in a narrative search for coherence and the sense of 'becoming' Miller described earlier. At other times, we are in a state of equilibrium, more concerned with 'being' and living out for a time a script, either self-created or societally provided.

In our interviews across a wide range of subjects and fairly long time periods, however, life storytellers did seem to follow a dominant mode of narrativity. In most interviews, most of the time, elaborators sought to elaborate and theorize their lives, while describers broadly kept close to a recognizable and fairly constant script which they described.

There are, though, some cases where the movement between types can be seen quite distinctly and for some people there is not a dominant type. Whilst they represent a small group, it is important to define these 'hybrid' narrativists because they open the debate about how narrative styles are developed and for many become embedded.

In the hybrid group, we see a group of people who move, sometimes spontaneously and instructively and in a succession of ages and stages, between the descriptive and elaborative modes of narration. We can see how age and social location play important roles in contextualizing narrativity. Narrativity may mediate between structure and agency, but the role of social positioning can be clearly evidenced. Social location is related to the resources and facilities that allow different kinds of narrativity to emerge and consolidate.

It is therefore worth exploring in some detail the small group we call 'hybrid narrators'. They illustrate the social complexity that underpins the different kinds of narrativity. Whilst we would not call this a hierarchy of narrativity à la mode of Maslow, there is certainly a pattern which relates to the topography of social relations. This is particularly well illustrated in the details of Armand's life story.

Armand is a fascinating case because the major transition in his life coincided with the four-year research period. He is interviewed about his country of birth just before he starts his new life, beginning from nothing, in a new country, England. He stories this process of 're-selfing' throughout the course of the interviews. We are able to see the life stages that his narrativity passes through. Rather than follow his father as a traditional tribal leader, he judges that his tribe's interests will be most judiciously served by undertaking a campaign of political activism and dissidence.

His narrativity and reflexivity can be discerned even in the period before he comes to England. With his father's death he is displaced from his script of an apprentice tribal leader in East Africa and begins to imagine other lives and to confront different realities. 'I went now to reality life,' he says. In this period, he is 'always thinking' and defining new courses of action. He develops a course of action based on political dissidence in his own country.

However, this activism is problematic. His wife wants him to abandon his quest to realize his socio-political dreams but he continues. In the event, he ends up being imprisoned for his activities. He escapes but goes on to find out that in all probability his wife and children have been killed. He escapes to a neighbouring country and then to Britain, where he seeks asylum in 2004.

This period of trauma leaves him feeling at first in Britain, 'like a baby'. At this time, his narrativity is highly descriptive and focussed on basic facts. This descriptiveness is related to a need to 'just live for the day'. When he thinks more deeply, it is so distressing that he feels suicidal.

Gradually, though, we see in the interviews how he begins again to restore his sense of selfhood, 'a small light comes on', and how he begins to think and indeed plan positively again. 'I was thinking about how to be very powerful now in my mind now because I lost (a) very deep thing?' He therefore defines a course of action, a 'dream' of a new life:

> This is the only one thing who keep me strong, me alive, keep me really in good condition with this dream. 'Cause I have to build it may be when I build it I will forget everything happened.

We can see in the detail from the interviews how Armand moves from descriptive episodes into periods of intense narrative activity and the personal elaboration of courses of action. We can see also how social contexts are implicated in the varying landscape of narrativity. At other points, Armand returns to descriptive recounting.

The traumas that Armand has experienced (father's death, imprisonment, loss of wife and children) have disrupted his quest for a macro-narrative of political involvement and transformation and for a time he struggles to survive. Upon arriving in Britain, he returns to being a more survival-led strategist with an associated descriptive narrative. As he settles and consolidates his social location somewhat, his narrative returns to a 'quest', 'a dream' of what his life could be like.

What these traumas and recoveries in Armand's life highlight is how social locations affect our narrativity. He moves from elaborative mode to 'living for the day' description and then back again to elaboration.

Roland is another case of hybridity without the dramatic transitions experienced by Armand. In Armand's case, it might be argued that the very complex of traumas in his life have contributed to a hybrid response as he confronts multiple settings and dilemmas. It is possible that this hybrid is less internally generated than externally imposed. From the beginning, Roland said he had 'multiple selves'. In the interviews, although there were some continuities, he did indeed present different versions of his narrative. Sometimes he was entirely descriptive, at other times markedly elaborative. Interestingly, he seldom mixed these modalities within a particular interview. He tended to be either one thing or the other. He was, in fact, the only one of our life storytellers who asserted that he had no essential self, but 'merely a set of different selves'.

The patterns of hybridity and multiplicity in the three, or possibly four, cases we interviewed are characterized by episodic change. But the sample and the narrative characteristic are so poorly represented that any generalization must be treated as very tentative. Perhaps what is most significant is the incredibly small number of life storytellers of this sort.

Most certainly, then, some people do work with a multiplicity of narratives with a shifting terrain for their ongoing identity projects. Moreover, even in the case of those with a more monolithic narrative character, either as elaborators or describers, there is some movement between categories over time (see Figure 11.1).

Narrativity

- Episodic reflexivity – periods of vision and periods of suspension.
- Process of 'becoming somebody' becomes uncompleted or suspended.
- Periods of 'floating' – rather that repositioning a sense of core identity.
- Some movement from original script, but episodically – episodic self-belief when in periods of 'becoming' and elaboration.

Styles of learning

- In episodes of elaboration, for a time this group resembles the autonomous. But these periods do not last.
- So in periods of engagement the elaboration drives the learning, but when in suspension learning is more disengaged and/or instrumental.

Repositioning, flexibility of response and self and personal development echo these episodic patterns.

Figure 11.1   Hybrid narratives

This having been said, most of our life storytellers held to a dominant style of narrative character. This underpinning narrative character provided the key to understanding how they approached and recounted the transitions and critical events in life, as the previous four chapters show. The narrative character provides the key as to how events will be integrated into the life narrative. Far from an embracing of multiplicity and an endlessly shifting sense of selfhood, the overwhelming majority of life storytellers were engaged in a search for coherence and continuity. Perhaps we face one of the many paradoxes of post-modernity that in a rapidly changing world of flux and flexibility people employ their narratives to provide an anchor, a sense of stability, continuity and coherence in a world of fast and often bemusing change.

This, then, was a way that people may have deployed and employed their narratives. But post-modern theorists are profoundly correct to point out the dilemmas and delusions involved in the process. For instance, in the 'American Dream' you can become whatever you dream or wish or narrate, as the Obama or Clinton narratives epitomize. This grandiose narrative vision is often, however, a delusion, and, moreover, most life narratives do themselves involve competing and contradictory forces within each account. It is also true that in such a fast changing and complex world, the search for an overarching sense of coherence and continuity is likely to remain distinctly elusive: the narrative quest that we find life storytellers engaged in is thus a long and challenging journey.

To show how this journey proceeds and how transitions are negotiated in ways that echo the search for continuity and coherence, we shall return to the case of Christopher, whom we met in Chapter 10. For it is in the moments of movement between different life events that we can see the assertion and reassertion of narrative character. Much of our work in the research projects reported here focussed on transitions such as critical learning episodes (the Learning Lives project) or migration (the Diasporas project). Hence, we were able to observe the flux and fluidity of post-modern life events. These transitions overwhelmingly evidenced how people held onto their dominant narrative character as they built and modified their life narrative.

Once again, the focus is on 'moments' or on 'movement' between different contexts or learning episodes, or in the case of our Diaspora studies, countries. In these movements, we see how people reposition their projects of self and identity. McAdams describes 'selfing' in this way:

> The process of selfing involves constructing and authoring experience as one's own, as well as appropriating, synthesising, reflection on and simply observing experiences in such a way that it is deemed to be mine. Over time, selfing builds up and attempts to build together the Me.
>
> (McAdams 1996: 302)

We refer to the repositioning of the self through narrative construction as 're-selfing'.

These points of renegotiation of the life narrative primarily reassert the dominant narrative character of the life storyteller. In a few cases, as we have seen, they exhibit a multiplicity of narrative impulses and perhaps a sense of multiple selfhood. Rather as Logan Mountstuart says in *Any Human Heart*: 'Every human being is a collection of selves we change all the time. We never stay as one person as we go on our journeys to the grave' (Boyd, 2010). But although this is logically true, our evidence points to a more sustained search for narratives of coherence and continuity and constancy and dominance of a particular narrative character for each person.

This search can be clearly seen in the passages on Christopher in Chapter 10. Here, we see a life storyteller coming to the end of his life and painstakingly analysing the costs and benefits of the way he has lived his life. He understands why he has spent so much time on elaboration, but as he moves to a new episode and a new version of life balance, it is once again through focussed elaboration that his narrative quest is pursued. He himself judges that his journey has a constant and consistent 'process of becoming' underpinning it. Throughout his life, the narrative has provided an anchor for an open exploration of spirituality and sexuality. To repeat his words: 'My journey seems to be towards some kind of fulfilment, some kind of completeness, some kind of togetherness with myself and the world.'

Such a journey understood in this way will most likely employ and deploy the narrative to play an integrative role. His conceptualization of his journey acts together with his desire for coherence and completeness, and his focussed elaboration follows this line of intent consistently.

The 'new mornings' he describes in his last interview represent new episodes in his life, but his desire is for a coherent self to play its role in the new context. He talks of this ongoing process of becoming and of a 'new self', a 'new Christopher' who will continue in the last phase of his life to define himself and delineate courses of action as he has done throughout what he calls 'his journey'. He will 're-self' for the new context, but he will use the habitual pattern of focussed elaboration to do that.

Exploring notions of reflexivity, re-selfing and hybridity allows us to see the kind of narrative journeys that people embark upon. Christopher's journey is an *open* narrative of becoming. He provides an example of how focussed elaboration is employed and deployed in the various critical incidents and transitions of life to re-self and provide an integrative narrative that searches for some kind of completeness. This process of elaboration develops from a life theme – his vocation of puppeteer – which he develops from the age of seven for nearly 60 years to the present. Understanding this life theme is an ongoing elaboration of his narrative that allows him to 'locate' and theorize his life. During his narrative journey, he comes to understand the origins of his life theme and pursue it through a range of vicissitudes of time and place. This life theme, this 'theory of life', develops his sense of self and identity and provides the narrative resources for the engagement with transitions and critical episodes which we tentatively call 're-selfing' – the 'new self', the 'new Christopher' he pursues at such times. Through his focussed elaborations he responds to the 'flexible' demands of modern life and counters the manipulation of self narratives that Cushman refers to in his analysis of the consumer society (1990). As Christopher re-selves, so he delineates new courses of action for each new context.

Multiple describers also move through these transitional moments, holding onto a consistent and coherent belief in prescribed scripts as their anchor and source of integration. They, too, follow an open trajectory, whilst employing closed scripts that are prescribed and focus on being rather than on becoming. Their lives provide openness and movement, whilst accepting the closure of prescribed scripts which themselves delineate clear courses of action and associated identity projects. George Johnson, one of our other life storytellers (Goodson 1996), embraces the scholarship boy storyline that we have referred to elsewhere. At 50, he finds himself following the same script in a new country, Canada, where he has migrated to make a new start. But his new start, his would-be retelling, draws on the same narrative of the scholarship boy. In the life history interviews, he began to 'locate' this script and to painstakingly theorize his life – a process he constantly asserts is now 'too late'. He says: 'I felt quite depressed, I realize that life has passed by. I was troubled by thoughts of what could have been.' His central dream was to become a professor or an eminent person who, crucially, would be announced over the tannoy at his home international airport in Central America. This, he felt, 'had driven him onwards'. But at 56 he sees that pursuing this script is patently pointless; he may get the PhD he is studying for, but it will only leave him unemployed in a foreign land. The closed nature of the script provides no flexibility and no viable courses of action.

> I now see the journey as a flight from self, or from destiny. Only by attending university could I be announced arriving at the airport … [now] … I don't really know whether I wanted that living out a culturally provided script.

Armchair elaborators, whilst intensively involved in narration and elaboration, do not develop open courses of action. High narrative intensity is repetitive and in that sense closed. The narration and elaboration moves, but in a circular and repetitive fashion, focussing again and again on similar events in the past and never integrating these into an account which leads on to open exploration of selfhood and a process of becoming.

Scripted describers have closed narratives and closed courses of action. From early on in life, a script is embraced which provides a lynchpin for all narrative construction. This script can provide contentment and coherence, but works best in stable unchanging contexts. Transitions and incidents prove huge challenges to the closed narrative, and as in the cases of John and May, present major life challenges because of the absence of flexibility. Untrained in the ongoing process of narrative construction, re-selfing proves hugely difficult, and flexibility of response is therefore circumscribed.

In the final chapter, we explore the issues of narrativity, learning and flexibility. In particular, we focus on how these issues will serve people in the new economic order that has emerged and been consolidated over the past two decades.

Chapter 12

Narrativity, learning and flexibility: towards the narrative future

In a way, the spectrum from description to elaboration covers a range from a more factual, vernacular narration of the world to a more theoretical or reflexive view. Richard Hoggart has written autobiographically about this impulse, which he sees as the capacity to theorize his life and imagine it differently. He describes this as a phenomenon in relation to the class-based society in which he grew up:

> Almost all working class people have been used to living as if subject to merely successive events. If the assault has a pattern it is that of birth and growth and death, it is that of seasons and main dates of the year and of the weekly wage packet. Working class life has long been dominated by the thisness of things and events and people; an unordered thisness.
>
> What almost all working-class life – almost all levels of life – avoids or, better, is unaware of, is intellectual pattern-making, generalising across and about habits in space and time, and so of gathering such generalisations together and hazarding judgments [...] To generalise about them is strange and can be disconcerting.
>
> (Hoggart 1990: 213–214)

Hoggart's own life story is wonderfully elaborated and he has written of his capacity to theorize his life to see it in context and in our terms to locate it. Above all, in reference to his characterization of working-class life he sees his exceptionality as 'a push for meaning outside the day to day' (ibid.: 89), a capacity to theorize his own life.

This capacity to 'theorize' and 'locate' our life story may provide a highly developed resource for responding flexibly to life events. Given the current demand for 'flexible' skills and 'flexible' labour, and given the potency and fluency of what Bauman calls 'liquid modernity', this narrative capacity may be of considerable import in the social conditions and relations emerging under globalization in late modernity. Bauman characterizes the contemporary scene in this way:

> An unprecedented fluidity, fragility and in-built transience (the famed 'flexibility') mark all sorts of social bonds which but a few dozen years ago combined into a durable, reliable framework inside which a web of human interactions

could be securely woven. They affect particularly, and perhaps most seminally, employment and professional relations. With skills falling out of demand in less time than it takes to acquire and master them, with educational credentials losing value against their cost of purchase by the year or even turning into 'negative equity' long before their allegedly lifelong 'sell-by' date, with places of work disappearing with little or no warning, and with the course of life sliced into a series of ever shorter one-off projects, life prospects look increasingly like the haphazard convolutions of smart rockets in search of elusive, ephemeral and restless targets, rather than a predesigned and predetermined, predictable trajectory of a ballistic missile.

(Bauman 2003: 91)

In the concluding part of this chapter, we look into the future to speculatively view patterns and perspectives as they might impinge on life narratives. In the emerging world of rapid communication and change, where people have to change jobs and partners with greater regularity, the cartography of life narratives will itself no doubt respond and possibly transform existing patterns. Certainly, the self project and associated life narrative would seem to require greater flexibility in the delineation of courses of action and may require what I call 're-selfing' at more regular intervals.

In his final novel, Malcolm Bradbury ruminated on the endless pursuit of selfhood. He wrote:

For the truth is that, though the self may be an anxious item, and we are all no more than a face drawn in the sand or on the very edge of the waves in a collapsing cosmos, the self as we've invented and pampered it, the private self, the personal self, is a being worthy of treasuring.

(Bradbury 2000: 426)

Whilst he 'invents and pampers' his self, he is aware of the perilous and precarious nature of the process. He is reminded: 'How fragile a life is, how we try to hold onto a shape and meaning for it, and yet always finding it's drifted away' (ibid.: 411). This is at the heart of the paradox of the pursuit of cohesion and learning which is featured in different ways, but nearly always present, in the various kinds of life narratives we have scrutinized.

Life narratives vary considerably according to historical periods and cultural contexts, and for this reason we have provided examples from a variety of cultures. This had led some to argue that 'invented and pampered' self narratives are primarily a function of the late capitalist West. Geertz has, for instance, noted that:

The Western conception of the person as a bounded, unique, more or less integrated motivational and cognitive universe, a dynamic centre of awareness, emotion, judgement and action organised into a distinctive whole and set contractively both against other such wholes and against the social and natural background is … a rather peculiar idea within the context of world cultures.

(Geertz, quoted by Lifton 1993: 87)

Commenting on this view, Lifton makes the following point: 'This conception of self is pre-protean, and has probably not applied for some time in most of the West as well' (Lifton 1993: 88). He adds: 'Protean or otherwise the self requires a modicum of inner continuity and of coherence as well, but on its own personal and cultural terms […] The sources of coherence can vary. But however elusive and inchoate the effort, all are engaged in it' (ibid.: 88). Lifton is commenting on the 'age of fragmentation' that accompanies the death throes of modernism, a point that Bradbury makes about the modernist institutions and public spaces in which selfhood once sought its endless definition. He says: 'We feel real and whole, but nothing about our life does, not even the buildings or monuments we set up to spare us this sense of exile, the pain inside modernity' (Bradbury 2000: 411). The collapse of so many of the meta-narratives and storylines of modernization poses seismic challenges for people's identity projects and life politics. Richard Sennet has shown in *The Corrosion of Character: the personal consequences of work in the new capitalism* (1998) how this new context poses huge challenges for the younger generations. In a sense, they are thrown back into personal spaces and individual life projects as they search for meaning and, enduringly, for some kind of coherence.

Sennett speaks of his own epiphany at the Swiss mountain resort of Davos where, for the last few years, he has attended a winter meeting of the elite of business and political leaders. The World Economic Forum at Davos 'runs more like a court than a conference. Its monarchs are the heads of big banks or international corporations' (Sennett 1998: 66). But Sennett finds a dilemma at the heart of the proceedings, namely, that the regime is 'losing the battle for the hearts and minds' of ordinary people. In a peculiar and deeply disheartening way, it is almost a rerun of the way that the defeated communist regimes first lost the engagement and commitment of their own people before losing the global battle. Sennett comments:

> It therefore seemed to me, as I wandered in and out of the conference halls, weaved through the tangle of limousines and police, or the mountainous village streets, that this regime might at least lose its current hold over the imaginations and sentiments of those down below.
>
> (ibid.: 147)

Sennett argues that having studied new social and workplace patterns:

> One of the unintended consequences of modern capitalism is that it has strengthened the value of place, arousing a longing for community. All the emotional conditions we have explored in the workplace animate that desire; the uncertainties of flexibility; the absence of deeply rooted trust and commitment; the superficiality of teamwork; but most of all, the spectre of failing to make something of oneself in the world, 'to get a life' through one's work. All these conditions impel people to look for some other scene of attachment and depth.
>
> (ibid.: 138)

What we may be seeing, then, is the beginning of a substantial 'turning away' from one of the major sites of collective purpose and social engagement – the workplace, and especially the public service workplace. The other side of this movement is a 'turning towards' the individual, the personal, the consumable, the special interest, the private purpose. It is not quite as stark as 'there is no such thing as society' or that 'greed is good', but it represents a growing focus on the private world of the individual self.

In a general sense, it is a turning away from common pursuits and public purpose towards personal missions and private consumption. This kind of 'turning away' from the public and common purpose is often seen in societies that lack a legitimate moral mission. For instance, in South Africa during the period of apartheid:

> Many white bystanders who intellectually opposed apartheid adopted a passive opposition. They retreated into private life, cut themselves off from the news media, refused to talk politics with friends, and adopted an intense immersion in private diversions such as sport, holidays and families.
>
> (Marshall 2001: 9)

In his remarkable study of American life, Robert Putnam has documented a similar kind of atrophying of American public purpose. He contrasts the baby boomer generation, who emerged as a social and political force in the 1960s, with the contemporary 'Generation X'ers':

> Unlike boomers, who were once engaged, X'ers have never made the connection to politics, so they emphasise the personal and private over the public and collective. Moreover, they are visually oriented, perpetual surfers, multi-taskers, interactive media specialists. In both personal and national terms, this generation is shaped by uncertainty (especially given the slow growth, inflation-prone 1970s and 1980s), insecurity (for these are the children of the divorce explosion), and an absence of collective success stories – no victorious D-Day and triumph over Hitler, no exhilarating, liberating marches on Washington and triumph over racism and war, indeed hardly any 'great collective events' at all. For understandable reasons, this cohort is very inwardly focussed.
>
> (Putnam 2001: 259)

Putnam shows how, at every level in American life, social activities and public purposes are in dramatic decline. To employ the previous analogy with wildlife, the 'global warming' of globalization is destroying the existing social ecology at a dramatic and unprecedented rate. The changes have come within one generation, an incredibly short time span in human history.

> Middle-aged and older people are more active in organisation than younger people, attend church more often, vote more regularly, both read and watch the news more frequently, are less misanthropic and more philanthropic, are most interested in politics, work on more community projects, and volunteer more.
>
> (ibid.: 247–248)

Putnam notes the change affects the range of passions, purposes and meanings; yet not all social networks have atrophied. Thin, single-stranded, surf-by interactions are gradually replacing dense, multi-stranded, well exercised bonds. More of our social connectedness is one-shot special purpose and self-oriented.

Bauman characterizes the loss of meta-narratives and public purposes, and indeed of private meaning and coherence, as a condition of 'liquidity'. 'In lasting commitments liquid modern reason spies out oppression in durable engagement, it sees incapacity in dependency' (Bauman, quoted in Jeffries, 2007: 8). 'As a result', he says, 'the era of liquid modernity may be catastrophic for romantic notions of love' (ibid).

Bauman draws the following conclusion, but it needs to be analysed carefully:

> Rational conduct in such a world demands that the options, as many as possible, are kept open and gaining an identity which fits too tightly, an identity that once and for all offers 'sameness' and 'continuity', results in the closing of options or forfeiting them in advance.
>
> (Bauman 2003: 148)

The key qualifier in this statement is 'once and for all' – continuity may be desirable for significant periods, but the important issue is openness to new challenges and the capacity to respond flexibly. The key insight is to understand the difference between a determined and constrained notion of individuality, isolated and devoid of wider collective purpose, and individuality as a springboard for self-assertion and connection to wider social purpose. As Bauman says, there is a growing gap between individuality as fate and individuality as a practical capacity for self-assertion. In the present situation of liquid social forms we are thrown back, whether we like it or not (and there is much not to like), to selfhood as a key site of struggle. This search for selfhood and for a sustainable life politics will be conducted as our communal and public sense is demeaned, deconstructed and demolished. Hence, the capacity to respond flexibly, delineate new courses of action and broadly pursue what we might call *re-selfing* becomes a key concern.

In this sense, the different modalities of narrativity discerned herein pose differentiated prospects and challenges for the capacities needed for re-selfing. Interestingly, Bauman ends up with a sense that for individuality to be enabling in its capacity for selfing and re-selfing there must be a sense of overarching purpose. He says:

> It is not the overwhelming pressure of an ideal which they cannot live up to that torments contemporary men and women, but the absence of ideals: the dearth of [...] firmly fixed and steady orientation points, of a predictable delineation for the life itinerary.
>
> (ibid.: 43)

Again, Bauman requires careful reading. He is not saying we need a fixed identity, not even a continuous sense of coherence, but something much more distant and processual – a destiny, an ideal and some orientation points for the journey. As our narratives unfold and we relearn and re-self, this provides a reasonable open framework for exploration.

In this sense, the crucial distinction in the issue of narrative capacity is that between how people employ *open* or *closed* narratives. This is often a complex conundrum to analyse and understand. We have seen how scripted describers can often embrace a relatively closed script early in life, which sets clear parameters for the roles and routines of their lives. We have also seen how in their lives this reduces their capacity to flexibly respond to changes in their life circumstances. Their capacity to re-self according to new circumstances is therefore circumscribed by their narrative character and constructions.

Likewise, we have seen how focussed elaborators develop, deploy and employ an *open* narrative which is personally elaborated at the beginning but constantly evolving; to use Miller's phrase, 'constantly in the process of becoming'. Hence, from the beginning a capacity to develop a personally elaborated life story, and allied to this delineated courses of action, becomes part of the person's narrative character. This kind of narrativity constantly responds flexibly to events and builds in a regular pattern of 're-selfing' into the fabric of living and narrating their lives.

Yet the spectrum of description to elaboration, and from closed to open, is complex. The multiple describers learn to move between scripts both conceptually and often geographically. This very mobility requires itself a pattern of flexible response and a capacity to 're-self' in new social settings and geographical locations. Each script embraced may even be somewhat closed, through an open exploration of these scripts mobility, flexibility and re-selfing can be embraced, experienced and inscribed within each life story.

In contrary form, armchair elaborators are constantly 'in the process of becoming' and are in that sense open, but whilst always becoming they never, so to speak, arrive. They are often unable to 'seal the deal', to link their practised and persistent capacity to elaborate new narrative constructions to the delineation of achievable courses of action.

Whilst, then, the spectrum of open and closed narratives and descriptive and elaborative modes is helpful, it still begs the question about the identity potential, learning potential and action potential of each life story. By analysing life stories for their potential in these dimensions, we may come to understand how individuals can make adjustments – re-selfing adjustments – to the new social conditions emerging in the new flexible work economy. The old world of fixed social arrangements and ascribed social roles is being replaced by a world of rapid and immediate change. The new economic order and new technologies will call for new narrative responses, and in this book we see how different kinds of narrative character will crucially affect how people can and do respond to these challenges.

Forms of narrativity

The summaries of different narrative styles recounted in chapters 7–10 develop from analysis of interview data and subsequently developed portrayals. Often in our portrayals we juxtapose people's 'narrative intensity' against their propensity to elaborate a personal story and delineate a course of action. The word 'story' covers a wide range of symbolic mental constructs from 'dreams', 'visions', 'self-images', 'personal myths' through to fully fledged 'missions' or 'projects' or 'life programmes'.

The groups in chapters 8 and 10 cover different modes of elaboration. One group comes higher up the 'food chain' in defining a life project, in some cases linked to a clear vocation from which they earn a living. This group we have called focussed elaborators. The word 'autonomy' captured some of their common aspirations: this urge to 'break out' from background and origins, to leave the pre-ordained social script and carve out a new original script. In fact, each person, whilst creating their own script, to some degree employs a range of existing scripted resources. As one interviewee said in an early project:

> My psychic projects have always been learned from 'fragments', 'embers' – that's how I build a sense of self. Idealized visions, glimpses, polestar figures, mentors – bits and pieces really … It is the construction of self as magpie, as bricolage, as collage. Building the self as a 'coat of many colours'.

Significantly, we can see how this act of self-invention draws heavily on pre-existing models and scripts. Hence, whilst the search may be for autonomy and independence, for, in a sense, escape, the existing 'social script' still maintains a hold.

This is also true in the associated realm of 'learning style'. Some learning the interviewees talk about is conventional and instrumental, employing existing educational resources. Other learning is more genuinely 'narrative learning' – linked to the ongoing elaboration of a life story and the linked delineation of courses of action.

Much of this latter learning is narrative learning because it is learning in the service of the identity project that is being storied and narrated. Figure 12.1 summarizes the main characteristics of focussed elaborators; what is significant here is that an open, personally crafted narrative is allied to an ongoing, open and flexible delineation of courses of action. The life narratives of focussed elaborators maximize the action potential, learning potential and identity potential available for life history construction.

The group in Chapter 8 are also elaborators, but we can discern a more tenuous link to the development of courses of action; these are above all armchair elaborators (Figure 12.2). By this, we mean that high narrative activity seldom translates into agentic behaviour – into the delineation of clear courses of action – which then command commitment. The degree of narrative intensity is sometimes enormous, even at times frightening. But armchair elaborators often give the impression of 'spinning their wheels' – of going round and round in circles. In some narratives, the person returns again and again to an earlier problem – a flawed relationship with a parent, a cataclysmic divorce – which has left the person confused and seemingly rudderless. The response is often a persistent form of narrative reinterpretation and an attempt to try out new narrative identities. But this ongoing attempt to re-self seems to encounter a 'blockage' when the attempt is made to define an associated course of

---

Narrativity

- High narrativity and reflexivity.
- Personalized elaboration – clear personal vision and articulated and operationalized plans.
- Flexibility of response and repositioning well orchestrated and continuous throughout the life course. Recreate but use their 'core identity' as a result of a successful passage towards 'becoming somebody'.
- High personal investment and self-belief.

Learning styles

- Instrumental learning, e.g. to become a musician or a puppeteer.
- Learning also involved in the process of definition of a self, 'becoming somebody'. The process of identifying and inventing a self identity.
- Ongoing elaboration – episodic repositioning of the above role. Ongoing operationalization. All of these involving a learning process.
- The narrative and ongoing elaboration are primary and the learning, which is instrumental, follows that. The learning is in the service of the core identity.
- Personal development and self-development linked.

Figure 12.1   Focussed elaborators

action. In this sense, we call this group armchair elaborators, people with great narrative intensity and capacity but with a low capacity for defining the courses of action that would allow new narrative identity to flourish and become embedded. There is a willingness – even a desperation – to re-self, but minimized capacity to implement new narrative identity. There is, then, an open exploration of life narratives and a narrative playing with a wide range of alternative stories. But there is a closure, a blockage that acts against turning these narratives into action, into a systematic delineation of associated courses of action or the development of alternative identity projects (Figure 12.2).

The groups in chapters 7 and 9 are those who primarily recount their life stories descriptively. There are presentations of a range of facts linked together with brief, sometimes experimental, accounts of life. There is seldom evidence of much internal reflection, and often the life story presented is normally short and summary. Yet an important group of describers do have a sense of personal vision to which they append a course of action. This group we call multiple describers (Figure 12.3). Sometimes, the personal vision is quite individualized, a commitment to a particular vocation, or a vision of family life. At other times, it is more communal or civic, for example, a belief in 'gypsy identity' or the 'Romany way of life'. Figure 12.3 summarizes multiple describers.

Scripted describers have less 'narrative intensity' than other groups (Figure 12.4). They are unaccustomed to talking about, or it seems, thinking about their life. As a result, their life storytelling is somewhat 'stuttering' with a generally unrehearsed

Narrativity

- High narrativity and reflexivity.
- Ongoing personalized elaboration and personal narrative activity.
- This group aspires to independence and 'becoming', but are held back in their stories at least by original scripting or by generalized but poorly formulated visions such as: 'the independent rebel', 'the battling woman'.
- Inability to delineate courses of action.
- Low self-confidence and self-belief.
- Social position anomalous – sense of rebelliousness and reinterpretation. Some movement between groups.
- Flexibility of response and repositioning. Considerable narrative movement, but a sense of unelaborated drift or generalized discontent because of lack of agency.

Learning styles

- Learning is uncoupled from any personalized elaboration.
- Learning not related to new courses of action or the development of new identity projects.
- Learning is instrumental, but is used for delivering other people's plans – often, paradoxically, other people from whom autonomy is sought.
- In general, schooling was unsatisfactory, although considerable commitment to personal projects or specialisms was evidenced. Little enjoyment of school learning and in some senses positive dislike.
- Personal development. In most cases still locked at an early stage of the process of 'becoming somebody'.

Figure 12.2 Armchair elaborators

Narrativity

- Low to middling narrativity and reflexivity.
- Personalized elaboration – personal vision high. Choose to move from their original social or geographical location.
- In the process of 'becoming somebody'.
- Self belief – determined and confident – reflexibility of response. Good at repositioning and renegotiation of personal plans.

Learning styles

- Instrumental learning directed towards 'becoming somebody' in line with the elaborated goal.
- This goal is focussed on an occupational goal, somewhat narrowly defined – some strategic learning in pursuit of this occupational goal.
- No holistic narrative learning since no holistic goals or narration; and since little work has been put into holistic goals or narration.

Figure 12.3 Multiple describers

quality. The narrative is less about making sense of a life, rather more about ordering the experiences and factually describing that experience. Scripted describers have a strongly rooted sense of their identity, even when in some cases the storytellers are 'travellers'. When, however, change comes, it is dealt with inflexibly, for life as it is lived and known has been deeply rooted and routinized.

The following diagram (Figure 12.4) summarizes scripted describers:

Narrativity

- Low narrativity and reflexivity.
- Personalized elaboration – low personal vision.
- Personal commitment to, and ownership of, ascribed role high.
- Self belief – a sense of 'This is what I do,' 'This is who I am.' An ascribed role. Repositioning – broadly stays with the original script; very low flexibility of response.
- Narrative closure early on – closed to learning and to other imagined futures.

Learning styles

- Learning within the ascribed role.
- Sometimes occupational as with John 'the farmer'; sometimes social as with May 'the gypsy'. But the occupational and social roles direct the learning, which is primarily instrumental in kind.

Figure 12.4   Scripted describers

In reviewing chapters 7–10, it is very important to stress that these types of narrativity only represent the dominant mode that people adopt in telling their life stories. They are not totally pure, all or nothing categories. All people move somewhat between these narrative forms. Nonetheless, having talked at great length with our life story-tellers we tend to find that most people do follow a primary category – an elaborator elaborates most of the time, a describer describes most of the time. These different styles leave people very differentially equipped for new social and economic futures.

The complexity of the modern world has been highlighted by the complex positionality of narrative constructionism. We have pointed to one paradox of the post-modern condition: that in a world of multiple niche identities and rapid change people often use their narratives to 'anchor' their sense of self and provide continuity and coherence. As Bauman points out, continuity seeking has a kind of 'negative equity' to it, but he concedes – as do others – that a sense of coherent purpose, 'of firmly fixed and steady orientation points', is of enduring importance for narrative construction.

This comes close to some of the arguments of Adam Curtis deployed in his wonderful television documentaries *The Century of the Self* (2002b) and *The Trap* (2007). This work has influenced other commentators. Madeleine Bunting writes:

> What we have is a cacophony of individual narratives, everyone wants to be the author of their own lives, no one wants to be relegated to a part in a bigger story;

everyone wants to give their opinion, no one wants to listen. It's enchanting, it's liberating, but ultimately it's disempowering because you need a collective, not individual narrative to achieve change.

(Bunting 2009: 23)

Curtis points out that a key figure in the twentieth century was Edward Bernays, who advised corporations and American presidents on how to manipulate people's unconscious desires.

In Bernays' future you didn't buy a new car because the old one had burnt out; you bought one to increase your self-esteem, or a more low-slung one to enhance your sense of sex appeal [...] you didn't vote for a potential party out of duty, or because you believed it had the best policies to advance the common good; you did so because of a secret feeling that it offered you the most likely opportunity to promote and express yourself.

(Curtis 2002a: 5)

People's individual desires and narratives therefore advanced to a centre-stage position in the terrain of selfhood. This process has been acutely analysed by Christian Salmon in his book *Storytelling*, which purports to show 'the timeless human desire for a narrative form and how it is abused in the marketing mechanism behind politicians and products' (Salmon 2010: cover page).

Individual narratives, then, can be used to service the power of the corporations and the people who increasingly seek only to represent these corporations – namely, politicians. Moreover, new technologies sponsor individual niche identities in a similar fashion, but also in ways that can disempower as well as empower.

Because we are all plugging ourselves into one great electronic mind, we will gradually lose the sense of each being shut off in a private mental space [...] our mental sense will be out there and as with Facebook, everyone will have access to it.

(Booth 2008: 43)

In this way, patterns of selfhood are changing, and with it the very nature of human beingness. Once our narratives were reconstructed, at least in part, within the mental space of our internal conversations; now they are interactively negotiated in cyberspace. The centrality of individual narratives in the new politics, the economy and the new technological arena points to their absolutely vital role in negotiating our social future. This in itself is an argument for understanding our narrative characters more acutely and perfecting how we employ and deploy our narrative resources. As Sennett and Cobb wrote long ago: 'Fragmentation and divisions in the self are the arrangements consciousness makes in response to an environment where respect is not forthcoming as a matter of course' (Sennett and Cobb 1972: 214).

This is precisely and exactly the environment in which people now often live. In order to fight against this narrative seizure of the new world order, it is therefore vital that we understand our narrative capacities and resources. Our 'narrative capital' needs to be employed and deployed to link our personal narratives to narratives of wider social purpose. Moreover, our narrative capital will need to be deployed in the recurrent 're-selfing' that the new flexible economies will demand. In the new social future, our narrative capacities hold one of the keys to the shape our world will take.

References

Adams, T. (2002) 'How Freud got under our skin', *The Observer Review*, 10 March.

Anderson, N. (1923) *The Hobo*, Chicago: University of Chicago Press.

Andrews, M. (1991) *Lifetimes of Commitment: ageing, politics and psychology*, Cambridge: Cambridge University Press.

Armstrong, P. (1987) 'Qualitative strategies in social and educational research: the life history method in theory and practice', Newland Papers No. 14, Hull: School of Adult and Continuing Education, University of Hull.

Barrett, S. (ed.) (1906) *Geronimo's Story of his Life*, taken down and edited by S.M. Barrett, New York: Duffield.

Bauman, Z. (2001) *The Individualised Society*, Cambridge: Polity Press.

Bauman, Z. (2003) *Liquid Love*, Cambridge: Polity Press.

Becker, H. (1970) *Sociological Work: method and substance*, Chicago: Aldine.

Bernays, E. (1924) *Propaganda*, New York: Liveright.

Bertram, M. (2005) 'In interview with David Cameron', *The Guardian*, 15 May.

Booker, C. (2006) *The Seven Basic Plots: why we tell stories*, London: Continuum International Publishing Group.

Booth, M. (2008) 'The book is dead. Long live Facebook!' *The Independent*, 13 January.

Boyd, W. (2010) *Any Human Heart* directed and written by W. Boyd, http://www.channel4.com/programmes/any-human-heart, Channel 4 Online (accessed 27 February 2012).

Bradbury, M. (2000) *To the Hermitage*, London: Picador.

Branigan, T. (2005) 'Kennedy prepares for the next step', *The Guardian*, 20 May.

Bronk, R. (2009) *The Romantic Economist: imagination in economics*, Cambridge: Cambridge University Press.

Bunting, M. (2009) 'Market dogma is exposed as myth. Where is the new vision to unite us?' *The Guardian*, 28 June.

Caldwell, C. (2005) 'The final round for party politics', *The Financial Times*, 19–20 November.

Campbell, D. (1996) Wayne on a Warm Day, Review of 'Bad Business' by Dick Hobbs, London Review of Books, 20 June.

Csíkszentmihályi, M. (1991) *Flow: the psychology of optimal experience*, New York: Harper and Row.

Csíkszentmihályi, M. and Beattie, O.V. (1979) 'Life themes: a theoretical and empirical exploration of their origins and effects', *The Journal of Humanistic Psychology*, 19 (1), winter.

Curtis, A. (2002a) 'How Freud got under our skin', *The Observer Review*, 10 March.

Curtis, A. (2002b) *The Century of the Self,* TV documentary series directed and written by Adam Curtis, BBC Four.

Curtis, A. (2007) *The Trap*, TV documentary series directed and written by Adam Curtis, BBC Two.

Cushman, P. (1990) 'Why the self is empty: toward a historically situated psychology', *American Psychologist*, 45 (5), 599–611.

De Beauvoir, S. (1972) *The Coming of Age*, London and New York: Norton & Co.

Denzin, N. (1989) *Interpretative Biography*, London: Sage.

Denzin, N. (1991) 'Deconstructing the biographical method', paper presented at American Educational Research Association Conference, Chicago, 9 April.

Didion, J. (2008) 'A fateful election', *The New York Review*, 25 October.

Dollard, J. (1949) *Criteria for the Life History*, Magnolia, MA: Peter Smith.

Emin, T. (2007) 'My life in a column', *The Independent*, 23 November.

Flores, F. and Gray, J. (2000) *Entrepreneurship and the Wired Life: work in the wake of careers*, London: Demos.

Garton Ash, T. (2008) 'The more Obama is tested, the more he shows his presidential mettle', *The Guardian*, 23 October.

Geertz, C. (1973) *The Interpretation of Cultures: selected essays*, New York: Basic Books.

Goodson, I.F. (ed.) (1992) *Studying Teachers' Lives*, London and New York: Routledge.

Goodson, I.F. (1996) 'Scrutinizing life stories: storylines, scripts and social contexts', in D. Thiessen, N. Bascia and I. Goodson (eds) *Making a Difference about Difference*, 123–138, Canada: Garamond Press.

Goodson, I.F. (2003) *Professional Knowledge, Professional Lives: studies in education and change*, Maidenhead and Philadelphia: Open University Press.

Goodson, I.F. (2004) 'Narrative capital and narrative learning', paper given to a workshop at the University of Viborg in November. This paper was considerably extended in doctoral classes given at the University of Barcelona in a course on life stories during the period January–July 2005.

Goodson, I.F. (2005) *Learning, Curriculum and Life Politics*, London: Routledge.

Goodson, I.F. (2008) *Investigating the Teacher's Life and Work*, Rotterdam, Boston and Taipei: Sense.

Goodson, I.F. and Ball, S. (1985) *Teachers' Lives and Careers*, London, New York and Philadelphia: Falmer.

Goodson, I.F., Biesta, G., Tedder, M. and Adair, N. (2010) *Narrative Learning*, London and New York: Routledge.

Goodson, I.F. and Gill, S. (2011) *Narrative Pedagogy*, New York: Peter Lang.

Goodson, I.F. and Hargreaves, A. (1996) *Teachers' Professional Lives*, London, New York and Philadelphia: Falmer.

Goodson, I.F. and Hargreaves, A. (2003) '*Change Over Time? A Study of Culture, Structure, Time and Change in Secondary Schooling*', USA: The Spencer Foundation.

Goodson, I.F. and Lindblad, S. (eds) (2010) *Professional Knowledge and Educational Restructuring in Europe*, Rotterdam, Boston and Taipei: Sense.

Goodson, I.F. and Sikes, P. (2001) *Life History Research in Educational Settings: learning from lives*, Buckingham and Philadelphia: Open University Press.

Goodson, I.F. and Walker, R. (1991) *Biography, Identity and Schooling*, London, New York and Philadelphia: Falmer.

Graham, R. (2004) 'Thinker, Writer, Soldier, Spy', *Financial Times Weekend*, 27/28 November.

Harrison, J.F.C. (1995) *Scholarship Boy: a personal history of the mid-twentieth century*, London: Rivers Oram Press.

Hoggart, R. (1990) *Uses of Literacy: working class life*, London: Chatto & Windus.

Jeffries, S. (2007) 'To have and to hold', *The Guardian*, G2, 20 August.

Kermode, F. (1967) *The Sense of an Ending: studies in the theories of fiction*, Oxford: Oxford University Press.

Knightley, P. (1998) 'Cool lives in the last days of love and marriage', *Sunday Times*, 18 October.

Lambert, R. (1968) *The Hothouse Society: an exploration of boarding-school life through the boys' and girls' own writings*, UK: Weidenfeld & Nicolson.

Lasch, C. (1977) *Haven in a Heartless World*, New York: Basic Books.

Lifton, R.J. (1993) *The Protean Self: human resilience in an age of fragmentation*, New York: Basic Books.

McAdams, D. (1996) 'Personality, modernity, and the storied self: a contemporary framework for studying persons', *Psychological Inquiry*, 7 (4), 295–321.

McAdams, D. (2001) 'The psychology of life stories', *Review of General Psychology*, 5 (2), 100–122.

McEwan, I. (1997) *Enduring Love*, London: Vintage.

McEwan, I. (2005) *Saturday*, London: Penguin.

Macintyre, A. (1981) *Virtue: a study in moral theory*, London: Gerald Duckworth & Company Ltd.

Marshall, G. (2001) 'Comment', *The Observer*, 28 October (see climate changes: http://www.risingtide.org.uk (accessed 28 February 2012).

Maslow, A. (1954) *Motivation and Personality*, New York: Harper Row.

Menaud, L. (1991) 'Man of the people', a review of *The True and Only Heaven* by C. Lasch, *New York Review of Books*, XXXVIII (7), 11 April.

Miller, J. (2010) *Crazy Age: Thoughts on Being Old*, London: Virago Press.

Munro, P. (1998) *Subject to Fiction: Women Teachers' Life History Narratives and the Cultural Politics of Resistance*, Buckingham: Open University Press.

Obama, B. (1995) *Dreams of My Father*, New York: Three Rivers Press.

Obama, B. (2006) *The Audacity of Hope*, New York: Crown Publishers, Random House.

O'Hagan, S. (2005) 'Boss class', *The Observer Magazine*, 24 April.

Putnam, R. (2001) *Bowling Alone: the collapse and revival of American community*, New York: Simon & Schuster.

Raban, J. (2008) 'He won but by what means?' *The Guardian*, 8 November.

Radin, I. (1920) 'Crashing thunder', *Publications in Archaeology and Ethnology*, 26, 381–473.

Richardson, J.G. (ed.) (1986) *The Handbook of Theory and Research for the Sociology of Education*, Westport, CT: Greenwood Press.

Robinson, J. (2007) 'Gloves come off as Mirror and Cameron declare war', *The Guardian*, 10 June.

Sage, L. (1994) 'How to do the life', review of *Writing Dangerously: Mary McCarthy and her world* by C. Brightman, *The London Review of Books*, 10 February.

Sage, L. (2001) *Bad Blood*, UK: Fourth Estate.

Salmon, C. (2010) *Storytelling: bewitching the modern mind*, London and New York: Verso.

Scott Peck, M. (1978) *The Road less Travelled: a new psychology of love, traditional values and spiritual growth*, London: Arrow Books.

Semprun, J. (2004) 'Interview', *Financial Times Weekend*, 27/28 November.

Senge, P. (1995) *The Fifth Discipline*, New York: Doubleday.

Sennett, R. (1998) *The Corrosion of Character: the personal consequences of work in the new capitalism*, London and New York: WW Norton.

Sennett, R. and Cobb, J. (1972) *The Hidden Injuries of Class*, New York: Knopf.

Shaw, C. (1930) *The Jack-Roller*, Chicago: University of Chicago Press.

Small, H. (2007) *The Long Life*, Oxford: Oxford University Press.

Solomons, J. (2009) 'Cinema's a very shocking tool. You must ask yourself what you're using it for', *Observer Film Magazine*, 6 December.

Steedman, C. (1986) *Landscape for a Good Woman*, London: Virago Press.

Thresher, F. (1928) *The Gang: a study of 1313 gangs in Chicago*, Chicago: University of Chicago Press.

Troy, G. (1999) 'Prosperity doesn't age well', *The New York Times*, 24 September.

University of Brighton and University of Sussex (2006–2009) 'Cultural geographies of counter-diasporic migration: the second generation returns "home"', Arts and Humanities Research Board funded.

University of Brighton, University of Exeter, University of Stirling, University of Leeds (2003–2008) 'Learning lives: learning, identity and agency in the life course', ESRC funded. http://www.learninglives.org/index.html (accessed 28 February 2012).

University of Brighton, University of Gothenburg, National and Kopodistorian University of Athens, University of Joensuu, University of Barcelona, University of the Azores, St. Patrick's College Dublin City University, University of Stockholm (2003–2007) 'Professional knowledge in education and health: restructuring work and life between state and citizens in Europe' (PROFKNOW), EU funded, http://www.ips.gu.se/english/Research/research_programmes/pop/current_research/profknow (accessed 28 February 2012).

Walker, R.M. (2008) 'A page has turned', *The Guardian*, 6 November.

Williams, H. (2005) *A Chronology of World History*, London: Cassell.

Willinsky, J. (1989) 'Getting personal and practical with personal practical knowledge', *Curriculum Inquiry*, 3 (19), 247–264.

Wirth, L. (1928) *The Ghetto*, Chicago: University of Chicago Press.

Zorbaugh, H. (1929) *The Gold Coast and the Slum: a sociological study of Chicago's north side*, Chicago: University of Chicago Press.

Recent publications on narrative studies by Ivor F. Goodson

Books

—— (1992) *Studying Teachers' Lives*, London and New York: Routledge.

—— (2000) *Livshistorier – kilde til forståelse av utdanning*, Bergen, Norway: Fagbokforlaget.

—— (2001) *Life Histories of Teachers: understanding life and work*, Japan: Koyo Shobo.

—— (2001) *The Birth of Environmental Education*, P.R. China, East China: Normal University Press.

—— (2003) *Professional Knowledge, Professional Lives: studies in education and change*, Maidenhead and Philadelphia: Open University Press.

—— (2003) *Väd är Professionell Kunskap? Förändrade Värdingar av Lärares Yrkesroll*, Sweden: Studentlitteratur.

—— (2005) *Learning, Curriculum and Life Politics: the selected works of Ivor F. Goodson*, Abingdon: Taylor & Francis.

—— (2007) *Politicas do Conhecimento: vida e trabalho docente entre saberes e instituições* (Organização e tradução: Raimundo Martins e Irene Tourinho), Brazil: Coleção Desenrêdos.

—— (2007) *Professional Knowledge, Professional Lives*, Beijing: Beijing Normal University Press.

—— (2007) *Professionel Viden. Professionelt Liv: studier af uddannelse og forandring*, Denmark: Frydenlund.

—— (2008) *Investigating the Teacher's Life and Work*, Rotterdam, Boston and Taipei: Sense.

—— (2009) *Developing Professional Knowledge about Teachers*, Hangzhou: Zhehiang University Press.

—— (2010) *Through the Schoolhouse Door*, Rotterdam, Boston and Taipei: Sense Publishers.

—— (2011) *Life Politics: conversations about education and culture*, Rotterdam, Boston and Taipei: Sense Publishers.

—— (2011) *The Life History of a School*, New York and London: Peter Lang.

—— and Ball, S. (eds) (1984) *Defining the Curriculum: histories and ethnographies*, London, New York and Philadelphia: Falmer.

—— and Ball, S. (eds) (1985) *Teachers' Lives and Careers*, London, New York and Philadelphia: Falmer.

—— and Ball, S. (eds) (1989) *Teachers' Lives and Careers*, London, New York and Philadelphia: Falmer/Open University, Open University Set Book Edition.

——, Biddle, B.J. and Good, T.L. (eds) (2000) *La Enseñanza y los Profesores, III, la Reforma de la Enseñanza en un Mundo en Transformación*, Barcelona: Ediciones Paidós Ibérica.

——, Biesta, G.J.J., Field, J., Macleod, F. *et al.* (2011) *Improving Learning Through the Life Course*, London and New York: Routledge.

——, Biesta, G.J.J., Tedder, M. and Adair, N. (2010) *Narrative Learning*, London and New York: Routledge.

—— and Gill, S. (2010) *Narrative Pedagogy*, New York: Peter Lang.

—— and Hargreaves, A. (eds) (1996) *Teachers' Professional Lives*, London, New York and Philadelphia: Falmer Press.

—— and Lindblad, S. (eds) (2010) *Professional Knowledge and Educational Restructuring in Europe*, Rotterdam, Boston and Taipei: Sense.

——, Loveless, A. and Stephens, D. (eds) (2012) *Explorations in Narrative Research*, Rotterdam, Boston and Taipei: Sense Publishers.

—— and Numan, U. (2003) *Life History and Professional Development: stories of teachers' life and work*, Lund: Studentlitteratur.

—— and Sikes, P. (2001) *Life History Research in Educational Settings: learning from lives*, Buckingham and Philadelphia: Open University Press.

—— and Sikes, P. (2006) *Life History in Educational Settings*, Japan: P. Koyoshuto.

—— and Walker, R. (1991) *Biography, Identity and Schooling*, London, New York and Philadelphia: Falmer.

Chapters in Books

—— (1983) 'Life histories and teaching', in M. Hammersley (ed.) *The Ethnography of Schooling*, Driffield: Nafferton.

—— (1985) 'History context and qualitative method', in R.C. Burgess (ed.) *Strategies for Educational Research*, London, New York and Philadelphia: Falmer Press.

—— (1988) 'Putting life into educational research', in R. Webb and R. Sherman (eds) *Qualitative Studies in Education*, 110–122, London, New York and Philadelphia: Falmer Press.

—— (1989) 'Understanding/undermining hierarchy and hegemony – a critical introduction', in A. Hargreaves *Curriculum and Assessment Reform*, 1–14, Milton Keynes and Philadelphia: Open University Press.

—— (1990) 'Teachers' lives', in J. Allen and J. Goetz *Qualitative Research in Education*, 150–160, Atlanta: Nova Science Publishers.

—— (1992) 'Dar voz ao professor: as historias de vida dos professores e o seu desenvolvimento profissional', in A. Novoa (ed.) *Vidas de Professores*, Coleccao Ciencias Da Educacao, Portugal: Porto Editora.

—— (1992) 'Laroplansforskning: mot ett socialt konstruktivistiskt perspektiv', in S. Selander (ed.) *Forskning om Utbildning*, 136–155, Stockholm/Skane: Brutus Ostlings Bokforlag Symposion.

—— (1992) 'Studying teachers' lives: an emergent field of inquiry', in I.F. Goodson (ed.) *Studying Teachers' Lives*, 1–17, London and New York: Routledge.

—— (1992) 'Studying teachers' lives: problems and possibilities', in I.F. Goodson (ed.) *Studying Teachers' Lives*, 234–249, London and New York: Routledge.

—— (1993) 'Sponsoring the teacher's voice', in M. Fullan and A. Hargreaves (eds) *Understanding Teacher Development*, London: Cassell and New York Teachers' College Press.

—— (1993) '"Un pacte avec le diable" ou des éléments de réflexion à l'intention des formateurs de maîtres', in *L'université et le milieu scolaire: partenaires en formation des maîtres*, Actes du troisième colloque, 3–21, November, Montreal: Université McGill.

—— (1995) 'Basil Bernstein and aspects of the sociology of the curriculum', in P. Atkinson, B. Davies and S. Delamont (eds) *Discourse and Reproduction*, Cresskill, New Jersey: Hampton Press.

—— (1995) 'The context of cultural inventions: learning and curriculum', in P. Cookson and B. Schneider (eds) *Transforming Schools*, 307–327, New York and London: Garland Press.

—— (1996) 'Representing teachers: bringing teachers back in', in M. Kompf (ed.) *Changing Research and Practice: teachers' professionalism, identities and knowledge*, London and New York and Philadelphia: Falmer Press.

—— (1996) 'Scrutinizing life stories: storylines, scripts and social contexts', in D. Thiessen, N. Bascia and I. Goodson (eds) *Making a Difference About Difference*, 123–138, Canada: Garamond Press.

—— (1996) 'Studying the teacher's life and work', in J. Smyth (ed.) *Critical Discourses on Teacher Development*, London: Cassell.

—— (1996) 'The personal and political', in T. Tiller, A. Sparkes, S. Karhus and F. Dowling Naess (eds) *Reflections on Educational Research: the qualitative challenge*, Landas: Caspar Forlag A/S.

—— (1996) 'Towards an alternative pedagogy', in S. Steinberg and J. Kincheloe (eds) *Taboo, The Journal of Culture and Education*, autumn.

—— (1997) 'Action research and the reflexive project of selves', in S. Hollingsworth (ed.) *International Action Research: a casebook for educational reform*, London and Washington: Falmer Press.

—— (1997) 'Holding on together: conversations with Barry', in P. Sikes and F. Rizvi (eds) *Researching Race and Social Justice Education – essays in honour of Barry*, Troyna, Staffordshire: Trentham Books.

—— (1997) 'New patterns of curriculum change', in A. Hargreaves (ed.) *A Handbook of Educational Change*, Netherlands: Kluwer.

—— (1997) 'The life and work of teaching', in B. Biddle, T. Good and I. Goodson (eds) *A Handbook of Teachers and Teaching*, 1 and 2, Netherlands: Kluwer.

—— (1997) 'Trendy theory and teacher professionalism', in A. Hargreaves and R. Evans (eds) *Beyond Educational Reform*, Buckingham (UK) and Philidelphia (USA): Open University Press.

—— (1998) 'Storying the self' in W. Pinar (ed.) *Curriculum: Towards New Curriculum Identities*, London and New York: Taylor & Francis.

—— (1999) 'A crise da mudança curricular: algumas advertências sobre iniciativas de reestruturação', in L. Peretti and E. Orth (eds) *Século XXI: Qual Conhecimento? Qual Currículo?* 109–126, Petrópolis, Brazil: Editora Vozes.

—— (1999) 'Entstehung eines Schulfachs', in I. Goodson, S. Hopmann and K. Riquarts (eds) *Das Schulfach als Handlungsrahmen: vergleichende Untersuchung zur Geschichte und Funktion der Schulfächer*, 151–176, Cologne, Weimar, Vienna, Böhlau: Böhlau-Verlag GmbH & Cie.

—— (1999) 'Representing teachers', in M. Hammersley (ed.) *Researching School Experience: ethnographic studies of teaching and learning*, London and New York: Falmer Press.

—— (1999) 'Schulfächer und ihre Geschichte als Gegenstand der Curriculumforschung im angelsächsischen Raum', in I. Goodson, S. Hopmann and K. Riquarts (eds) *Das Schulfach als Handlungsrahmen: vergleichende Untersuchung zur Geschichte und Funktion der Schulfächer*, 29–46, Cologne, Weimar, Vienna, Böhlau: Böhlau-Verlag GmbH & Cie.

—— (2000) 'Professional knowledge and the teacher's life and work', in C. Day, A. Fernandez, T.E. Hauge and J. Møller (eds) *The Life and Work of Teachers: international perspectives in changing times*, London and New York: Falmer Press.

—— (2001) 'Basil Bernstein F. 1925–2000', in J. Palmer (ed.) *Fifty Modern Thinkers on Education: from Piaget to the present*, 161–169, London and New York: Routledge.

—— (2002) 'Afterword – international educational research: content, context, and methods', in L. Bresler and A. Ardichvili (eds) *Research in International Education: experience, theory, with practice*, 180, 297–302, New York: Peter Lang.

—— (2004) 'Change processes and historical periods: an international perspective', in C. Sugrue (ed.) *Curriculum and Ideology: Irish experiences, international perspectives*, Dublin: The Liffey Press.

—— (2005) 'The personality of change', in W. Veugelers and R. Bosman (eds) *De Strijd om het Curriculum*, Antwerpen/Apeldoorn: Garant (sociology of education series).

—— (2006) 'Socio-historical processes of curriculum change', in A. Benavot and C. Braslavsky (eds) *School Knowledge in Comparative and Historical Perspective: changing curricula in primary and secondary education*, Comparative Education Research Centre, Hong Kong: The University of Hong Kong.

—— (2008) 'Procesos sociohistóricos de cambio curricular' in A. Benacot and C. Braslavsky (eds) *El Conocimiento Escolar en una Perspectica Histórica y Comparativ: cambios de currículos en la educación Primaria y Secundaria*, in *Perspectivas en Educación*.

—— (2008) 'Schooling, curriculum, narrative and the social future', in C. Sugrue (ed.) *The Future of Educational Change: international perspectives*, 123–135, Routledge: Abingdon.

—— (2008) 'The pedagogic moment: searches for passion and purpose in education', in *At Sætte Spor en Vandring fra Aquinas til Bourdieu – æresbog til Staf Callewaert*, Denmark: Forlaget Hexis.

—— (2009) 'L'interrogation des réformes éducatives: la contribution des études biographiques en éducation', in J.-L. Derouet and M.-C. Derrout-Bresson (eds) *Repenser la justice dans la domaine de l'éducation et de la formation*, 311–330, Berlin, Brussels, Frankfurt am Main, New York, Oxford, Vienna: Peter Lang.

—— (2009) 'Listening to professional life stories: some cross-professional perspectives', in H. Plauborg and S. Rolls (eds) *Teachers' Career Trajectories and Work Lives*, 3, 203–210, Dordrecht, Heidelberg, London and New York: Springer.

—— (2009) 'Personal history and curriculum study', in E. Short and L. Waks (eds) *Leaders in Curriculum Studies: intellectual self-portraits*, 91–104, Rotterdam, Boston and Tapei: Sense.

—— (2012) 'Case study and the contemporary history of education', in J. Elliot and N. Norris (eds) *Curriculum, Pedagogy and Education Research: the work of Lawrence Stenhouse*, London and New York: Routledge.

—— and Ball, S. (1985) 'Understanding teachers: concepts and contexts', in S. Ball and I. Goodson (eds) *Teachers' Lives and Careers*, London and Philadelphia: Falmer Press.

—— and Cole, A. (1993) 'Exploring the teacher's professional knowledge', in D. McLaughlin and W. G. Tierney (eds) *Naming Silenced Lives*, 71–94, London and New York: Routledge.

—— and Gill, S. (2011) 'Life history and narrative methods', in B. Somekh and C. Lewin (eds) *Theory and Methods in Social Research*, 2nd edition, Los Angeles, London, New Delhi, Singapore, Washington DC: Sage.

—— and Walker, R. (1995) 'Telling tales', in H. McEwan and K. Egan (eds) *Narrative in Teaching, Learning, and Research*, 184–194, New York: Teachers College Press.

Technical Reports

—— (1991) 'Studying teacher's lives: problems and possibilities' from the project 'Studying Teacher Development', London, Ontario: Faculty of Education, University of Western Ontario.

—— (1999) 'Studying the teacher's life and work', in P. Kansanen (ed.) 'Discussions on some educational issues VIII, Research Report', Volume 204, Helsinki, Finland: Department of Teacher Education, University of Helsinki.

——, Biesta, G., Field, J., Hodkinson, P. and Macleod, F. (2008) 'Learning lives: learning, identity and agency in the life course', The Economic Research Council [Reference: RES-139-25-0111].

——, Fliesser, C. and Cole, A. (1990) 'Induction of community college instructors', from the Interim Report of the project 'Studying Teacher Development', 50–56, London, Ontario: Faculty of Education, University of Western Ontario.

—— and Mangan, J. (1991) 'An alternative paradigm for educational research', from the project 'Studying Teacher Development', London, Ontario: Faculty of Education, University of Western Ontario.

——, Mangan, J. and Rhea, V.A. (eds) (1990) 'Teacher development and computer use in schools', Interim Report No. 4 from the project 'Curriculum and Context in the Use of Computers for Classroom Learning', London, Ontario: Faculty of Education, University of Western Ontario.

Monographs

——, Biesta, G.J.J., Tedder, M. and Adair, N. (eds) (2008) 'Learning from life: the role of narrative', Learning Lives summative working paper, University of Stirling: The Learning Lives project.

—— and Mangan, M. (eds) (1991) 'Qualitative studies in educational research: methodologies in transition', RUCCUS Occasional Papers, 1, 334, University of Western Ontario.

—— and Mangan, M. (eds) (1992) 'History, context, and qualitative methods in the study of education', RUCCUS Occasional Papers, 3, 279, University of Western Ontario.

——, Müller, J., Hernández, F., Sancho, J., Creus, A., Muntadas, M., Larrain, V. and Giro, X. (2006) 'European schoolteachers' work and life under restructuring: professional experiences, knowledge and expertise in changing contexts' for the ProfKnow Consortium, Brighton: University of Brighton.

—— and Norrie, C. (eds) (2005) 'A literature review of welfare state restructuring in education and health care in European contexts: implications for the teaching and nursing professions and their professional knowledge' for the ProfKnow Consortium, Brighton: University of Brighton.

Journal Articles

—— (1980–1981) 'Life histories and the study of schooling', Interchange, 11 (4).

—— (1986) 'Stuart's first year', New Era, August.

—— (1990) 'Laronplansforskning: mot ett socialt konstruktivistiskt perspektiv', Forskning om utbildning, 1, 4–18.

—— (1991) 'Sponsoring the teacher's voice', Cambridge Journal of Education, 21 (1), 35–45.

—— (1992) 'Investigating schooling: from the personal to the programmatic', New Education, 14 (1), 21–30.

—— (1993) 'Forms of knowledge and teacher education', in P. Gilroy and M. Smith (eds) International Analyses of Teacher Education, Jet Papers 1, Abingdon, Oxfordshire: Carfax.

—— (1993) 'The Devil's bargain', Education Policy Analysis Archives (electronic journal), 1 (3).

—— (1994) 'From personal to political: developing sociologies of curriculum', Journal of Curriculum Theorizing, 10 (3), 9–31.

—— (1994) 'Qualitative research in Canadian teacher education: developments in the eye of a vacuum', International Journal of Qualitative Studies in Education, 7 (3), 227–237.

—— (1994) 'Studying the teacher's life and work', *Teaching and Teacher Education*, 10 (1), 29–37.

—— (1994) 'The story so far: personal knowledge and the political', *Resources in Education*, ERIC Issue RIEMAR95, I.D.: ED 376 160.

—— (1995) 'A genesis and genealogy of British curriculum studies', *Curriculum and Teaching*, 9 (1), 14–25.

—— (1995) 'Education as a practical matter', *Cambridge Journal of Education*, 25 (20), 137–148.

—— (1995) 'Storying the self: life politics and the study of the teacher's life and work', *Resources in Education*, ERIC Issue RIEJAN96, I.D.: 386 454.

—— (1995) 'The story so far: personal knowledge and the political', *International Journal of Qualitative Studies in Education*, 8 (1), 89–98.

—— (1996) 'Towards an alternative pedagogy', *Taboo, The Journal of Culture and Education*, autumn.

—— (1997) 'Action research and the reflective project of self', *Taboo, The Journal of Culture and Education*, spring.

—— (1997) 'Representing teachers', *Teaching and Teacher Education: An International Journal of Research and Studies*, 13 (1).

—— (1997) 'Trendy theory and teacher professionalism', *Cambridge Journal*, 27 (1), 7–22, spring.

—— (1998) 'Preparing for post-modernity: storying the self', *Educational Practice and Theory*, 20(1), 25–31.

—— (1999) 'Professionalism i reformtider', *Pedagogiska Magasinet*, 4, 6–12, December.

—— (1999) 'The educational researcher as a public intellectual', *British Educational Research Journal*, 25 (3).

—— (2000) 'Life histories and professional practice', *Curriculum and Teaching*, 16 (1).

—— (2000) 'The principled professional', *Prospects*, UNESCO, Geneva, January, 181–188.

—— (2001) 'Med livet som innsats (faktor)', *Bedre Skole: Norsk Lærerlags Tidsskrift for Pedagogisk Debatt*, Oslo, 1, 49–51.

—— (2001) 'Social histories of educational change', *Journal of Educational Change*, 2 (1), 45–63.

—— (2001) 'The story of life history: origins of the life history method in sociology', *IDENTITY: An International Journal of Theory and Research*, 1 (2), 129–142.

—— (2002) 'De la historia al futuro: nuevas cadenas de cambio Entrevista a Ivor Goodson', *Revista Páginas de la Escuela de Ciencias de la Educación U.N.C.*, 2 (2) and 3, 9–17, Córdoba, September.

—— (2002) 'La personalidad de las reformas', *Cuadernos de Pedagogía*, 319, 34–37, December.

—— (2002) 'Un curriculum para una sociedad democrática y plural Entrevista con ... Ivor Goodson', *KIKIRIKI*-62/63, 25–30, September 2001/February 2002.

—— (2003) 'Hacia un desarrollo de las historias personales y profesionales de los docentes', *Revista Mexicana de Investigacion Educativa*, VIII (19), September–December.

—— (2004) 'Onderwijsvernieuwers vergeten de leerkracht', *Didaktief*, 34 (3), March.

—— (2005) 'The exclusive pursuit of social inclusion', *Forum*, 47 (2), 145–150.

—— (2006) 'The reformer knows best, destroying the teacher's vocation', *Forum*, 48 (3), 253–259.

—— (2007) 'All the lonely people: the struggle for private meaning and public purpose in education', *Critical Studies in Education*, 48 (1), 131–148, March.

—— (2007) 'Currículo, narrativa e o futuro social', *Revista Brasileira de Educação* 12 (35), May/August.

—— (2007) 'Questionando as reformas educativas: a contribuição dos estudos, biográficos na educação' (Dossiê Temático: Em Multiplicidades nomeia-se currículo, organizado por Antonio Carlos Amorim), *Pro Posições*, 8, No. 2 (53), 17–38, May/August.

—— (2010) 'Times of educational change: towards an understanding of patterns of historical and cultural refraction', *Journal of Educational Policy*, 25 (6), 767–775.

—— and Adlandsvik, R. (1999) 'Møte med Ivor F. Goodson', *Norsk PEDAGOGISK ttidsskrift*, 82 (2) 96–102.

—— and Anstead, C. (1993) 'Structure and mediation: glimpses of everyday life at the London technical and commercial high school, 1920–40', *American Journal of Education*, 102 (1), 55–79.

—— and Anstead, C. (1995) 'Schooldays are the happiest days of your life', *Taboo, The Journal of Culture and Education*, 11, 39–52.

—— and Anstead, C. (1998) 'Heroic principals and structures of opportunity: *conjoncture* at a vocational high school', *International Journal of Leadership in Education*, 1 (1), 61–73, January.

—— and Baraldi, V. (1999) 'Entrevista, Ivor Goodson with V. Baraldi', *Revista El Cardo*, UNER, Year 2, 2 (2), 29–31.

—— and Cole, A. (1994) 'Exploring the teacher's professional knowledge', *Teacher Education Quarterly*, 21 (1), 85–106.

—— and Fliesser, C. (1994) 'Exchanging gifts: collaborative research and theories of context', *Analytic Teaching*, 15 (2).

—— and Fliesser, C. (1995) 'Negotiating fair trade: towards collaborative relationships between researchers and teachers in college settings', *Peabody Journal of Education*, 70 (3), 5–17.

—— and Fliesser, C. (1998) 'Exchanging gifts: collaboration and location', *Resources in Education*, February.

—— and Foote, M. (2001) 'Testing times: a school case study with M. Foote', *Education Policy Analysis Archives*, 9 (2), January (http://epaa.asu.edu/epaa/v9n2.html), accessed 28 February 2012.

—— and Hargreaves, A. (2006) 'The rise of the life narrative', *Teacher Education Quarterly*, 33 (4), 7–21.

—— and Mangan, J.M. (1996) 'Exploring alternative perspectives in educational research', *Interchange*, 27 (1), 41–59.

—— and Mangan, J.M. (1996) 'New prospects/new perspectives: a reply to Wilson and Holmes', *Interchange*, 27 (1), 71–77.

——, Moore, S. and Hargreaves, A. (2006) 'Teacher nostalgia and the sustainability of reform: the generation and degeneration of teachers' missions, memory, and meaning', *Educational Administration Quarterly*, 42 (1), 42–61.

——, Muller, J., Norrie, C. and Hernandez, F. (2010) 'Restructuring teachers' work-lives and knowledge in England and Spain', *Compare: A Journal of Comparative and International Education*, 40 (3), 265–277, May.

—— and Norrie, C. (2009) 'Les enseignants de demain: perspective anglo-saxonne sur la restructuration des vies professionnelles et des connaissances des enseignants du primaire', *Des enseignants pour demain, éducation et sociétés*, edited by Patrick Rayou, No. 23 (1), 153–168.

—— and Numan, U. (2002) 'Teacher's life worlds, agency and policy contexts', *Teachers and Teaching: Theory and Practice*, 8 (3/4), 269–277, August/November.

—— and Pik Lin Choi, J. (2008) 'Life history and collective memory as methodological strategies: studying teacher professionalism', *Teacher Education Quarterly*, 35 (2), 5–28.

——, Sikes, P. and Troyna, B. (1996) 'Talking lives: a conversation about life', *Taboo, The Journal of Culture and Education*, 1, 35–54.

Index

1960s 7

action focus 69
Adams, T. 13
Age of Enlightenment, the 12
agency 8, 69, 70, 7; and action 69
America 23, 89, 90; underclass 28
American 90; academic scholarly society 28, 36; dream 28, 115; history 28; life 121; public purpose 121; rock star 12; social activities 121; society 28, 29
Anderson, N. 32
Andrews, M. 29, 94
Anglo-American context 81
Anglo-American cultural milieu 71
Annalistes 31
apartheid 121
Armand 113–14
Armstrong, P. 30
Arthur Miller Centre for American Studies 64
Arts and Humanities Research Board 8
Audiard 25
Australia 89
Austro Hungarian Empire 41
autonomy 29, 38, 96, 97, 108, 124; nationalist 11; personal 21

baby boomer 31; generation 121
Ball, S. 4
Barrett, S. 32
Bauman, Z. 24, 118–19, 122, 127
Beattie, O.V. 57–8, 97
Beauvoir, S. de 65
Becker, H. 32, 33
Beckham, D. 11
Beckham, V. 11
Beijing Normal University 27
Bergen-Belsen 43

Bernays, E. 13, 128
Bernstein, B. 69, 70
Bertram, M. 15
Biden, J. 16
Biesta, G. 41
Big Society, the 15
Booker, C. 3–4, 63, 79
Booth, M. 128
Boyd, W. 116
Bradbury, M. 119, 120
Branigan, T. 14
British Household Surveys 36
Bronk, R. 19
BSE 78
Bullingdon Club 14
Bunting, M. 128

Cameron, D. 14, 15
Campbell, D. 36
Canada 4–5, 91, 92, 93, 117
Canadian project 6
Canadian universities 6
capitalism 28; new 120; modern 120
Carré, J. le 74
case studies: detailed 71; personal 41
Catholic 41, 44, 102
Cauldwell, C. 13
Ceausescu 44, 45
Charles 92–3, 95
Chicago School of Sociology 32
Chile 51
China 25, 27
Christian 11, 13, 84; society 87; world 87
Christopher 98–111, 115, 116
Christou, A 95
class struggle 14
Clinton, B. 16, 115
Cobb, J. 128